It's a Long Way from China to Hollywood

Grace F. Yang
Ghostwritten by Sames

iUniverse, Inc.
Bloomington

It's a Long Way from China to Hollywood

iUniverse books may be ordered through booksellers or by contacting:

iUniverse
1663 Liberty Drive
Bloomington, IN 47403
www.iuniverse.com
1-800-Authors (1-800-288-4677)

ISBN: 978-1-4502-9659-5 (pbk)
ISBN: 978-1-4502-9660-1 (cloth)
ISBN: 978-1-4502-9661-8 (ebk)

Library of Congress Control Number: 2011902230

Printed in the United States of America

iUniverse rev. date: 06/28/11

For my family: You honor me

by always being there.

For my daughter, Yvonne Lu:

My best friend in life.

You bring me all the joy

and happiness in the world.

My father, my mother, and I in Zhengzhou, 1977

Contents

Foreword

America is a country of immigrants from all over the world. These days, more and more immigrants are arriving from Asia than ever before. But most of their personal stories will never be known outside of their families and close circle of friends.

One wonderful exception to this rule is this book, *It's a Long Way from China to Hollywood*, by my personal friend Grace Yang. Employing a very detailed and intimate approach to her and her family's journey from Communist China to America, Mrs. Yang, in a very engaging literary effort, tells her story to us as if we were members of her extended family. Once we finish reading her story, that is exactly how we feel.

Rather than writing in generalities about the circumstances of her life, Mrs. Yang relates to us in specific detail the events that molded her and her family's lives, displaying her personal and unique sensitivity to her journey and her powers of observation.

In the end, it becomes very clear that she wants us to understand that whatever level of success she has achieved, it has been attained through hard work and dedication. There have been no guarantees on her path, but plenty of love and determination.

We owe a deep debt of gratitude to Mrs. Yang for bringing us this book. In a way, it could be the story of many other immigrants who, in spite of many challenges, have found their own ways of overcoming life's obstacles. With this in mind, Mrs. Yang's book can bring us only timeless inspiration.

Wea H. Lee
Chairman/CEO
Southern News Group
ITV International Television
ITC International Trade Center
Houston, Texas
July 2010

Acknowledgments

I never thought about writing a book like this. I intended only to tell my daughter's story. If anything I have said offends anyone or hurts anyone's feelings, forgive me. That was never my intention. This is just one person's view and the memories of a little girl growing up. I am proud of what I have written, and of my family, and I feel honored to tell our story. In doing so, I found that I love America as much as I love China and that I'm torn between the two.

Grace

I never thought about writing a book. I have been a songwriter and performer most of my life. I met Grace and Yvonne in the summer of 2007. I became great friends with Grace and was intrigued by the fact that Yvonne has been working since she was five years old. Grace kept telling me she wanted to write a book about her daughter's success. We talked about it several times, until I finally agreed to help her with it.

It became so much more.

Sames

Congratulations

Congratulations to my beloved daughter on her first book

It takes ten years of hard work to grow a tree

But one hundred years of hard work to rear a person

Like a stick in a relay race that my father handed to me

I gave it to my only daughter

Who then passed it on to my only granddaughter

Who received the star of USA-Sina award

And has now been recognized by China and America

Your father
Bingli Yang

Old China—I am on the right

1:   The Mei Puo

It is May of 1964, in Henan Province, China, just outside of the city of Kaifeng. A young couple ride their bike up and down a narrow stone road. The woman is pregnant, past due. She is sitting on the back seat of the bike and holding her husband tightly. They hope that riding on the rough stone road will induce labor.

He has fifteen days of vacation. On May 8, he left Beijing. He picked up his wife in the city of XinXiang. They traveled three hundred miles to Kaifeng, where their parents live, arriving on May 10, so they could be with them when the baby is born.

It is now the evening of May 22. He will be leaving for Beijing the next morning at 7:00 a.m. Things have gotten desperate. If this baby doesn't come tonight, it will be almost a year old before he ever sees it. He'd thought he was coming home to see his new baby. Instead it seems like he is going to have to leave without seeing it at all.

Finally, resolving themselves to the fact that this baby is not coming tonight, he and his wife retire for the evening. Around 2:00 a.m., they wake with the bed soaked. Her water has broken. They walk to the hospital with her parents. The baby arrives just before 6:00 a.m. on May 23. He has just enough time to hold his new baby girl and kiss her tiny cheek before he is off and running for the train station.

That's how I was born.

My mother told me that three months later, she managed to take me to Beijing to see my father. She said she had me dressed in a traditional blue doupen outfit, with handmade red-tiger shoes and a red-dragon cap, because I was born in the year of the dragon.

My birth name is Yanyan Yang; Yanyan, loosely translated, means beautiful Beijing. I was an only child. My father and mother went to the same school. My mother was in her last year of middle school and my father was in his last year of high school when they met. They were both fifteen years old. In China, school is structured differently than in America. Before my mother's time, girls were not encouraged to go to school at all. It took my mother a long time to convince my grandparents to let her go to school. Girls were expected to stay at home, and learn how to be domestic. My mother told me that it was mostly my grandfather she had to fight with. It was 1955. My mother was the leader of girls' gymnastics, and my father was the leader of boys' gymnastics at their school.

My mother was lucky to even be attending school. China's new leader, Mao Zedong, had started the New Republic of China. When my mother was ten years old, girls were allowed to attend public school along with the boys. Before that, the only way a girl could go to school was if her parents could afford to send her to a private school for girls or to hire a teacher to come to their house. Both of these options were very expensive.

In China at that time, most marriages were prearranged. There was supposed to be a Mei Puo involved, which is basically a professional matchmaker. All couples were supposed to be brought together through the Mei Puo. If you weren't and got married anyway, your family would not accept your husband or wife. You would be considered shamed. You just were not supposed to go against your family in any way in those days. But my mother and father lived at a time when young people didn't want to go through the Mei Puo anymore. They had new ideas about a lot of things.

During my mother and father's time, there was no dating at all. The boy's family would go to the Mei Puo, who would then approach the girl's family. If her family agreed to the match, they would then be engaged to be married. They did not see each other until the night of their wedding. The bride would wear a piece of red cloth covering her entire head, so that the groom could not see her face. After a complete day of celebrating, which would usually start early in the morning, and after all the friends and family were gone, just the two of them would be left. Then the groom could remove the cloth from his new bride's head.

The morning after their first night together, the groom would show his parents a special piece of white cloth, revealing a red blood stain that showed that his new wife had indeed been a virgin. If he could not produce the white cloth, or if there was no stain on the white cloth, there would be an uproar between the families. The girl would be considered trash and sometimes would even be sent back to her family. At the very least, she would be looked upon terribly by her new in-laws.

My mother was considered a bad girl by some people in the community. When my grandfather found out my mother was dating my father, he actually put a gun to her head, ordering her to never see that boy again. My mother told me that story. She said it was one of the most traumatic moments of her life. She said that when my grandparents spoke to my father the first time, they scared him so badly that he disappeared for a while. My grandfather had a gun due to his position in the community; he had once formally held a high rank in the military. Not just anyone in China could get a gun.

I view my mother and father as heroes for thinking for themselves. They were in love with each other and did not want to go through the Mei Puo. Needless to say, my mother and father got married, and they have been married for forty-eight years. When my grandparents finally gave in, they still insisted on going through the Mei Puo so they could keep up appearances in the community.

My mother worked in Xinxiang City, and my father worked in Beijing; the cities are about five hundred miles apart, but on the train, it seemed like twelve hundred miles. The trains stopped everywhere along the way. In China at that time, when you graduated from college, the government assigned you a job. Those jobs were not always close to your loved ones. You had no choice but to go. My father worked six days a week and got vacation once a year. So I mostly stayed with my mother in Xinxiang City and saw my father for fifteen days each year until I was twelve years old.

The earliest thing I remember about my childhood is waking up before daylight with my mother to get on the back of a military truck to go visit my grandparents and relatives in another city. We traveled all kinds of ways when I was growing up: trains, bicycles, motorcycles, scooters, and carts drawn by horses, cows, or tractors.

My mother, a doctor, had all kinds of contacts. She would get us rides on vegetable trucks, mail trucks, all kinds of delivery trucks, and many military trucks. I hated the military trucks. They had flat beds with railings on the sides. Sometimes they had a canopy covering the top and sides. If we were lucky, we would get to ride up front. But more times than not, we ended up in the back.

During the winter, it was so cold. The wind cut through me like needles. The drivers always drove fast, and the roads were in poor condition.

I always held onto the railings until my hands were sore. In the winter, we could feel the trucks sliding on the icy roads.

They often stopped because of mechanical problems. Then we had to sit there and wait forever while I froze to death or baked in the heat. Sometimes it got worse and started pouring rain. The trucks didn't have batteries, so the drivers had to crank-start them. The worst was when they could not get the truck running again. Then we had to sit and wait for the next truck to come along, one that had enough room for us.

I think my mother chose the military most of the time because she trusted the military. But it didn't always work out, and when it didn't, it really sucked. It seems like my whole life I've been traveling; even back then we were always moving somewhere new, or I was going back and forth between my mother and father.

Once, when I was about six or seven years old, a truck broke down on us in the middle of a snowstorm. This one wasn't a military truck; I think it was a delivery truck. The snow was coming down hard, and it was hailing. There was no traffic on the road at all for a long time. I was so cold; I thought we were going to die there. My fingertips were red like tomatoes, and my toes were completely numb. Finally, a military truck showed up and got us started again, but my mom chose for us to ride with military.

The reason I was born in Kaifeng is that my mother and father went to be with their families when it was close to my delivery time. That is how they usually do it in China, so the family can take care of the mother and the new baby. My mother told me that for the first thirty days, the mother and baby were not allowed to go outside. So the family would take care of everything. That sounds logical to me. A lot of things about Chinese culture are very logical.

When I was a little girl, I had lots of dreams. I loved singing and dancing. Even though my mother was a doctor and my father was governor, my family was poor. Well, we weren't poor, but we lived in a Communist country. We had the same as everyone else. In fact, I think we had a little more than the average family.

II: Growing Up Communist

In China at that time, it didn't matter what your job or position in the community was; you still got paid the same as everyone else. If you were a mayor or governor like my father, your job may have gotten you more respect, but not more pay. Only with seniority would you get a little bit more pay. With my mother's and father's positions, I guess we were better off than most people. But everyone was pretty much equal in China at that time.

When I was five or six years old, my father bought ten baby chicks and one rooster so my mother and I could have eggs to eat. The only way you got food in China at that time was if you raised it yourself or if you had coupons from the government that you could use at the market.

The coupons allowed you to buy certain things, but only in certain amounts. Take meat, for example. If my family had a coupon for meat, we could buy one pound. If we had no coupon, we couldn't buy any meat. There were coupons for meat, eggs, tofu, material, household goods—just about everything. There wasn't enough for everyone, so they were rationing. Basically, China was paying back its debt to Russia. At least that was the rumor among us kids.

You got only a certain number of coupons depending on the size of your family. My family was just my mother and me. We never had enough, so my father got us the chickens. It was going to be my job to feed them. This was the first time I had seen my father in a year. I hardly knew him at all.

"Calm those chickens down before you go in there, Yanyan," my father yelled as I opened the door.

I couldn't have been more than six years old at the time, and I was scared. We had them in a pen, and I had to go inside it to feed them. All the chickens knew I had food. They pecked at my ankles and legs. They jumped on my head and bit my hair, and I dropped the pan of food. Right away, I could see the disappointment in my father's eyes. That was my first feeling of being ashamed.

"You have to be strong," he told me. "Don't ever be scared of them."

But I couldn't help it; I was scared of them. I was scared of everything at that age.

Every time I saw my father, it was a big deal for my mother. It was a big deal for me, too, but in a completely different way. She would start cleaning the house a month ahead of time. I would start getting nervous a month ahead of time. We both had to get dressed in our best clothes the day he arrived. Sometimes my mother made my clothes, and sometimes I wore hand-me-downs from my cousins. You couldn't just go to Kmart or Walmart and pick out a nice dress for yourself. Remember, this was Communist China in the sixties. There were no department stores, no malls.

We always went to the train station way too early. We would stand there and wait forever for the train. I would think to myself, *Who is this guy?* I barely even knew him. My mother was always so happy, singing and telling me all about my father.

I can see them in my mind right now, hugging and kissing at the train station. When he kissed me, I hated it. He had a beard that scratched my face, and he was so tall. I was just intimidated by him.

The whole time I was growing up, my father was like an uncle I had who lived far away. He was family, but he didn't live with us. It was a big deal when he arrived, but as soon as I got used to him being there, he would be gone again. It was one of the hardest things I had to deal with growing up. Some people thought I had no father.

When we went to the train station with him on the day he was leaving, my mother would start crying, and then I would start crying. I would cry because she was crying. My mother would cry for days afterward. I hated my father for a long time because of that. Years went by before I realized it had never been his choice.

Each time my father came home, he brought bright-colored material from Beijing for my mother to make clothes out of for me. In my city, and in most cities in China, you could get only solid green or solid blue, or gray if you were lucky. Sometimes he even brought patterned material.

6

My mother would use the different colors to patch the holes in my pants, skirts, and jackets.

Another good thing about my father coming home was that he would take us out to restaurants. Plus, he made different food at home than what my mother made. He had gotten some different recipes from Beijing. My father is a very good cook. When it was just my mother and me, we always ate at home. I don't ever remember my mother taking me to a restaurant. She is a good cook, but not nearly as good as my father. I've never been good at it.

My father would take us to a restaurant as soon as we left the train station after picking him up. "Are you hungry?" was always the first question he asked when he saw us. Unfortunately, I have to tell you that most of the time when I was growing up, I was hungry. It wasn't unusual for people to go a full day without eating in China back then.

My father would also take us to a restaurant before we dropped him off at the train station when he left. When I was growing up, going out to a restaurant was a really big deal, especially for a child my age. My friends would ask me what it looked like inside the restaurant and what kind of food they served there.

I can't remember ever seeing any other girls when I went to restaurants with my parents. I might have seen some boys, but it was mostly just adults.

Food was not in abundance at that time. Eating was always a problem. While I was growing up, people did not say, "How are you doing?" or "Good morning." Instead, "Have you eaten yet?" was the greeting of the day.

From the time I was born until I was twelve, my mother received thirty-four Chinese yuan a month from the government. At that time, that was about four American dollars. She also received food coupons, which were almost more valuable than money. You couldn't replace them. I remember my father made a special drawer for the coupons so my mother could keep them locked up. The whole time I was growing up, whenever my mother gave me money and coupons to go to the market, she would say, "Don't lose the coupons." She never said, "Don't lose the money." Of course, there was never much money anyway, but, like I said, there was no way to replace the coupons.

We never had enough money for extras. Communism isn't bad, though; we had no rent and no power bill, phone bill, or any other bill. We had no phone, no radio, no TV, no refrigerator, no microwave. Believe me, four dollars did not go very far. We used coal for heat and for cooking, which cost money too. We were lucky: my father got a coal press so we could make our own. You could buy the coal powder for a lot cheaper than you could buy the chunks of coal.

I used to have a great time pressing coal with my father. I would be covered from head to toe in black coal dust. Before we had the coal press, my father would take the powder in his hands and squeeze it as hard as he could to make a coal ball—that's what I called them. With the press, I had to hang my whole body from the handle so that I could use all of my weight to smash the coal.

"Come on, bounce on it, Yanyan," my father would encourage.

"Look at that," he would say, pulling the piece of coal from the press. "You did a great job. My little girl is so strong."

By the time the day arrived for him to go back to Beijing, he would have chunks of pressed coal stacked up for my mother and me to use while he was gone. I remember that when the coal ran out, I would try to make the pressed coal myself, but I couldn't.

Once I was crying when my mother came home, and she asked why.

"I had no problem pressing the coal before," I told her, "and now I can't."

"Don't you know your father helps you?" she said. "He pressed that coal before you ever started working on it, baby."

Then I really started crying, realizing how much I missed my father.

My father did so many things like that. He was trying to make things as easy as possible for my mother and me, because he was never there. These are some things I've realized as I've gotten older.

When I think back, it seems like my father didn't sleep in the fifteen days he was home each year. All he did was fix and make things for my mother and me. He knew he was going to be gone for the rest of the year. Now that I am older, I am so proud of my father, and I love him so much. He really made our lives a lot easier than I ever could have imagined as a child.

No matter what he did, though, it still didn't make up for the fact that he was gone most of the time. My mother still had to deal with everything by herself for the rest of the year. It was hard growing up without my father. My mother is a very diligent, strong woman with a lot of tenacity. She taught me so many things about life—spiritual things, personal things. My mother taught me like I was a girl, but my father taught me like I was a boy.

My mother would take the material my father brought from Beijing and make clothes for me. My mother was very good at this. The other kids probably thought we had money, because I would be dressed in such colorful clothes, but I would rather have had my father.

In China at that time, even if you saved up enough money, there were some things you just could not buy, because there was not enough for everyone. My mother told me that when she and my father got married, her parents searched everywhere for a hope chest, but there was not one to be found.

I had one toy during my childhood: a doll my father brought from Beijing. I was so proud of her. I named her Niuniu, which means baby girl. I was the only girl in my area who had a doll that wasn't homemade. I had the real thing. Her eyes opened; her head, arms, and legs moved; she had hair on her head; and she wore clothes. I had to hold onto her tightly, because the older girls would try to take her from me.

Every day, I would wash her face, comb her hair, and cut her fingernails. I had cut her fingernails so much that her fingers were gone. None of the older girls ever wanted to play with the younger girls, but they liked me because I had a doll. We were all so amazed by the fact that when I held her upright, her eyes were open, but when I laid her down, her eyes closed. Wow! We just thought that was the neatest. She had eyebrows and everything.

I was only around six years old at that time, and I was so excited that the older girls wanted to play with me. Then they wanted to play doctor. They said whoever had a baby doll would be a patient, and whoever didn't would be the doctors. They took my baby into another room to be examined. I waited outside for a long time, and then I finally went into the room. They had all of her clothes off, and they were trying to see how she was made.

"It's getting late. I have to go home," I told them.

"You can't take your baby home," one of the girls said. "She is very sick, so she will have to stay here."

I started to cry as I walked home without my baby. When I got home, my mother saw how upset I was. I told her what had happened.

"We're going back there to get your baby right now," she said. "Everything will be fine."

When we returned, the girls didn't have my baby. They told us that she'd been very sick and had died. Well, obviously my mother didn't believe them, but I did. I fell down on the floor and started screaming, "Oh, no, my baby, my baby …"

These girls were smart. They walked us outside to where they had made a small grave with a little plaque that read "Niuniu's Grave." My mother still wasn't buying it.

"There is no baby doll in that grave," my mother shouted. "Where is my daughter's baby doll?"

"She really died, and we buried her," one of the girls said. "You wouldn't want us to dig her up, would you?"

"If my daughter doesn't have her baby doll in her hands in the next few minutes, I will be talking to your parents," my mother told them.

Three of the girls stepped off to the side and started whispering. Then one of them walked inside the building and came back out with Niuniu in her hands. I ran up, grabbed her from the girl, and ran back to my mother. It wasn't the only time those girls tried to get her from me, though.

I had her for a couple of years. One day, we were playing hide-and-seek. I don't know exactly what happened, but it started raining really hard—it was a huge storm—and the next thing I knew, my baby doll was gone. I had hidden her from the other girls, but when I went to get her, she was gone. I never saw her again. I cried for many days. She was like my real baby, or my little sister; I was an only child. Sometimes I still miss her. It sounds stupid, but it's true.

My parents couldn't afford to replace her, but I did get two baby rabbits the next time my dad came home to visit. It wasn't the same, but at least it was something. I kept those rabbits for a long time. When they had baby rabbits, I would give them to my friends from school.

When you're young, you don't realize how bad things really are. You just think that's the way life is. I would probably still not know any difference if I hadn't traveled so far in my life. Come to think of it, compared to the standard of living in China at that time, I guess you could say we were wealthy.

The truth is, when I look back, I realize we were just surviving. I realize, however, that many people in the world had much worse childhoods than I had. My childhood was not bad at all, really. I had a very happy childhood. Only after experiencing different places and different things do I see things differently. I guess what I'm trying to say is that some people have it really bad, and some people have it really good, and I was raised somewhere right in the middle.

Now that I am an adult living in America, I realize—wow, how I realize. I know there are still children in China and in America who don't have enough food or any toys, clothing, or anything. People all over the world are suffering because of the greed that seems to control everyone.

My father gave me my first real responsibility in life. We barely had enough food to feed ourselves, and we never had anything to feed our chickens, rabbits, and ducks. Every day, I had to go to the market and pick discarded vegetables off the ground to bring home for the animals.

The first time my father took me to the market, but then he went back to Beijing. I was so shy and scared about going down there by myself. I felt like I was stealing. But I knew all the animals were depending on me. I was the only way they got food and water, unless my father was home. My mother did not feed the animals—that was my job.

When I was with my father at the vegetable stands, no one said anything; everyone was really nice. When I wasn't with my parents, however, adults treated me differently; I need say nothing more. I know my childhood was not perfect, but imagine families in China at that time who had more than one child. At least everything my mother and father did was for me and only me. I never had to share with brothers and sisters. I love my parents so much.

When I was little, I went to daycare in the hospital where my mother worked. They had a big, round, fenced-in area in which they would put all the kids to play. My mother was always the last parent to come at pick-up time. I was always so happy to see her that I would start running circles inside the fence when I saw her coming down the long hallway. I would go crazy until she finally picked me up.

The only time I was away from her was when she was working. But my mother worked a lot of hours. She was the last one picking up her child because she was coming out of surgery or held up at a meeting. She was always taking classes to become a better doctor. She was one of the head doctors at that hospital. Later in life, she told me that those pick-up times were some of her happiest moments of my childhood. When she saw me running in circles like that, so happy to see her, it didn't matter how tired or stressed she was—she said it all just went away.

As an adult, at my worst moments, when I'm weak, crying, and feeling sorry for myself, I feel just like I did when I was a little girl, waiting alone for my mother to pick me up from that playpen.

Another good thing about my father coming home was that I didn't have to go to daycare. I was with him all day, every day, for the whole fifteen days he was home. I told you that as soon as I got used to him being around, he would be gone again. I see now that I was my mother's only happiness and joy for a long time. She raised me practically by herself until I was thirteen.

My father came home just before I was to start first grade. He put a house key on a piece of blue material for me to wear around my neck.

"Now you're a big girl with responsibilities," he told me. "You're not at daycare anymore. You'll be going to school, so you need a house key."

The first or second week after I started first grade, my best friend, Xilin, and I were hungry. I had my house key, so we decided to walk all the way back home without telling anyone. We didn't even know we were supposed to tell anyone.

My mother was working at the hospital. The school contacted her and told her I was missing. Xilin's parents were also contacted. Then the police got involved. Everyone was looking for us. Meanwhile, we were at my house, eating and playing, with no idea that there was a big emergency. I was always doing something stupid like that. It was never anything big; it was always innocent. But it seems like not much time would pass before I found myself in another one of these situations.

The next time my father came home, I lost the house key he had made for me. He was so upset. "I want you to find that key, Yanyan," he shouted. "Don't come back home until you have it."

I looked everywhere I could think of until it was after dark. I was crying the whole time and scared to go home. My friend Xilin had been helping me look for it. When it got dark, even she started to cry. She felt so bad for me. Finally, she and her mother walked me home.

"I am hardly ever at home, and you are my only child," my father told me. "You have to be here for your mother. You need to learn more responsibility."

"I'm sorry. I will try harder," I told him as I started to cry again. He gave me a hug and put me to bed.

He had another key made and tied a heavy piece of metal on it so I could feel it hanging around my neck. He gave it to me at the train station when he was heading back to Beijing.

"I love you. You are my daughter, and I trust you," he told me. "I know you won't lose this key. You're a schoolgirl now. You're growing up."

I never lost that key. I'm glad I didn't; that would have been the worst thing ever. Now I think to myself how hard it was for him to get the money to make me a key for our house in the first place.

One time when my father was home, he told me to go across to the hospital to get hot water. We had a container that my mom always used, kind of like a Thermos but with a big cork lid. I took the container and went off to the hospital, so happy to be helping my daddy.

No one had water running in their house. The only place to get water in the whole complex of about fifty or sixty families was—and I'm not making this up—right in front of the door to our house. So the whole neighborhood came to my door all day long, every day.

I'm serious—all of this is true. It's too bad we couldn't have sold the water. We would have been rich. But even this water was cold. The only place to get hot water was the hospital, or you had to heat it at home, which would cost you fuel. The only reason we could go to the hospital was that my mom worked there.

Let me tell you why we had the hot-water container in the first place. Once a year, a government official would come around with a pot full of pieces of paper with something written on them. Each head of household would reach in and pick one. Whatever was written on the paper was what you got. This was always a really big deal for everyone. A lot of trading would go on that day, and my mother was always involved.

She would get a cooking pot and trade it for an umbrella for me to walk to school with. In my city, it rains a lot. She would trade to get material to make clothes. My mother was always making extra money or some kind of trade for making clothing for people.

This time she was so happy about getting a hot-water container. This was something no one had. You couldn't even buy them in the market. Everyone wanted to trade with her, but she held on tight to the container with one hand and grabbed my hand with the other, and we went home. My mother was so happy; we were singing and dancing. I didn't even really understand why she was so happy. I just knew she was happy, and that made me happy.

We hardly had anything. I didn't often see my mother get happy about something. When she did, it always made me extremely happy.

Once she got a flashlight the same way. It was the same situation. Everyone wanted to trade, but she wanted nothing to do with it. I think we were the only ones to ever have a flashlight in my whole complex. She has always been a shrewd businesswoman.

Anyway, I went off to the hospital with the container and filled it with hot water. On my way back, stupid, happy-go-lucky me lost the lid to the container.

This time my father really gave me a hard time. I felt so bad. I looked for that lid so many times, every time I walked that way, the entire time I lived in Xinxiang, until I was eleven. I used to think it would make my mom and dad so happy if I could just find that lid.

Now that I'm an adult, I realize that the lid didn't lay on the ground very long at all. You never really lost anything there; you dropped it, and the very next person who walked by picked it up. No one had anything extra. When you live like that, everything is usable. You can't blame the person who picked up the lid.

"When you're in the middle of doing something, you have to pay attention, Yanyan," my father told me. "It doesn't matter how happy you are or who you're talking to. The lid on the container pops off easier when there's hot water in it."

He said all of this after he yelled at me and made me cry. It didn't make me feel any better; I still had to tell my mom about it when she got home.

I was always screwing up in some way with my father. I loved him; I hated him; I learned so much from him. I was a nervous wreck every time he came home. No wonder I was always screwing up. I was trying to show him what I could do and make him proud of me, but in the end, I would just mess it up.

III: An Only Child

When I was four years old, my mother got pregnant. She also got ill, so I had to stay with my aunt and uncle for about three months. They lived in the mountains, far from my city. They worked for the government, in a factory, making military goods. I had a great time with my aunt and uncle. They had no children at the time, so they spoiled me. I loved it.

My mother had the baby at six months; I'm sure she wasn't eating right. This was during the Chinese Cultural Revolution, and my mother was a doctor. They were short on doctors, and she was working all the time. She was told that she would never have another child, which is something she probably knew anyway.

Once she was told this, though, she sent an emergency telegraph, telling my aunt and uncle that she wanted to see me right away.

My aunt and I climbed into the back of a truck with a bunch of other people. This was in China, in the sixties; there was no Greyhound bus route or anything like that. It was a military truck, of course. I was playing with another little girl and having fun, excited to see my mother and the new baby.

We were on a mountain road, and it was lightly raining. It was in the early morning, just after daylight.

"It's too dangerous," my aunt told me. "We need to sit in the front."

"Driver, can you please stop!" she shouted.

"What's wrong?" I asked her.

"Just grab your things, and bring your friend, too," she said. "We're going to ride in the front now."

We got in the front of the truck, along with the other little girl. Right after the truck started moving again, it went right off the side of the

15

mountain. I was little, and I don't know how far down the truck went. All I know is that I had glass in my face, and the other little girl had glass in her face. Blood and glass were everywhere.

I know my aunt spent a long time in the hospital afterward, and I know she saved my life that day. She, the other little girl, and I were the only ones who survived. Everyone else on that truck died, including the driver.

When my aunt and I didn't arrive at the hospital to see my mother and the baby the next day, my mother called my uncle to find out where we were. My uncle knew about the accident and knew that three people had survived. But he did not know who.

When he told my mother what had happened, they say she almost went into shock, saying, "My only child is gone. And I will never have another one."

When I arrived at the hospital three days later, my mother hugged me so hard I couldn't breathe. I thought she would never let me go.

"My baby, you're alive, you're alive," she kept saying. "I can't believe it."

I went to the maternity ward with my grandmother to see the baby. When we got there, I saw a lot of babies, more than twenty.

"Are these all my mother's babies?" I asked.

They pointed to a little tiny baby inside an incubator, with tubes hooked to it. It lived for only ten days. It was so tiny, they never even knew if it was a boy or a girl. I think my mother knew it was going to die. Once again, she cried for days.

I was so young then that I didn't even know what it meant when they said someone died. After that, though, I knew what they meant.

Now my father knew that I was going to be his only child, and he seemed to get even harder on me. I think my father had always wanted a son instead of a daughter. But I know my father loves me, and he would do anything for me.

I remember my mother used to do theater a lot. The first time she took me to one of her shows, it was a story about a poor family who sold their daughter to a rich family because they couldn't take care of her. The rich family tortured and beat her. My mother played the part of the poor girl.

I was so young that I didn't realize it was just a show. When I saw my mother looking so ragged and dirty, being sold to those people, I got really upset. When I saw them start beating her, and she was crying for her mother, I lost control. I was already sobbing, and the woman taking care of me was so into the show, she just kept telling me to be quiet. Now I started crying out for my mother, just like she was crying out for her mother on the stage.

"My baby is crying," my mother finally shouted from the stage.

The audience started to laugh. My mother thought it was really funny later, when she was talking about it.

When I was little, during Mao Zedong's time, once a week, everyone in my complex would come together and eat leaf soup and bread they had made with grass and leaves. This was mandatory. It was so we would remember the poor and hard times in the past.

I hated it. I thought it was stupid. We were living in the hard times and the poor times! I always thought it was crazy when they would say to remember the past.

If they were worse off in the past than we are right now, how did they survive? I would think to myself.

While we were eating, people would read from Mao's book over the loudspeakers. Sometimes the Cultural Revolution song would play. By the time I was six or seven, they were down to doing this once a month. By the time I was about nine or ten, they had stopped doing it altogether, thank God! I guess it was good for my education, though. But you would never have heard me say that back then.

Growing up, I always wanted to play an instrument. Every day in the early morning, three or four houses down from my house—or, I should say, my room, because it was one room with a kitchenette and no bathroom—I heard music playing. But let me digress for a moment. In our entire complex, there was only one restroom for men and one restroom for women. Each one had about seven or eight holes in the ground, with no partitions or anything. There was always a line. It was horrible. Back then, though, I didn't know it was horrible. I didn't even know what partitions in a restroom were. When that's all you've ever known, it seems completely normal. The first time I went into a regular restroom, I thought, *Now this is pure luxury*. I was maybe thirteen years old, and it was in Beijing.

Anyway, the boy three or four houses down from me played the violin every morning. On the other side of my house was a girl who played the Chinese harp. She was really good. We had no music, no radio, and no record player. I loved listening to them play. When our rooster crowed in the background, I pretended he was singing.

I asked my mother if I could play an instrument and take lessons like those kids did. My mother told me that even if we could afford to buy an instrument, she would not have the money to pay for a teacher or the time to take me there. She told me that since I liked to sing and dance so much, she would talk to the school to see if I could join the school's singing and dancing girls' group. They recruited girls only from the third grade and up. I was only in second grade.

"Look at my daughter—she is tall and mature for her age," my mother told them. "She's been singing and dancing since she could walk and talk."

They asked me to sing a song, so I did. I decided to sing a song about factory workers. At that time, we didn't have many songs except Chinese revolution songs. While I sang, I also danced. They liked it so much that they let me in the group. I was so happy, and I took every rehearsal seriously. This was the first big thing in my life besides my father coming home once a year. By that time, we were under Mao Zedong's rule. All workers had to donate a certain amount of their time to working in the villages. This was a time in China when the cities were reaching out to the rural areas and the farmers.

All the students, from the fifth grade and up, were sent to the villages and farms to help the farmers and learn how they lived and worked. My group was sent to sing and dance for the farmers in the spring, when they were planting the new crops. We sang a song to encourage them and to hope for a good harvest, as well as to thank them for being the ones who fed the people. I was so proud, because I was the youngest person there. This is one of the many things that make me realize that China and America could learn so much from each other.

Let me tell you what I did to get there. All students from the fifth grade and up had to start training for the military. Everyone in my singing group was in the fifth grade or up, except me. I was in the third grade by then. The school said that since I was so young, I did not have to participate in the whole thing. I told my mother that I wanted to do it, because I didn't want to let my group down, and I didn't want anyone thinking I was a baby.

My mother thought I was crazy; all the students would be marching there, and it was a long way.

"Do you think you can really do this, Yanyan?" she asked me. "I don't think you're big enough to walk all the way there."

"Yes, I can do it," I told her. "I want to wear the uniform and carry a canteen and backpack like everyone else."

"You don't know how far it is," she told me. "You're too young."

18

"I don't care," I said. "If I'm not there, there will be one person missing from our dance routines."

We argued back and forth until I finally won.

So my mother made a special blanket for me to hang on my backpack, because the standard one was too big and heavy for me.

While we were marching, soldiers and teachers kept asking me if I needed help. I was so proud of myself; I kept telling them no. By the time we got there, my feet were bleeding and blistered. They were hurting really badly. I didn't care, though. I sang and danced, just happy to be part of it all.

When I got home and my mother saw my feet, she was so mad at me that she started crying. "If you couldn't do it, you should have asked someone for help!" she yelled.

"But I did do it, Mom," I told her. "I marched all the way there and back with everyone else."

My feet ended up getting infected. I had a fever for an entire week. But I got a certificate from my school for being the youngest student to ever make that march.

Since I was doing so well in school, I received my red arm badge. If you have ever seen pictures of school kids in China, you've probably noticed some of them wearing a red scarf, which is worn around the necks of young pioneers, or younger ones wearing a red arm badge.

I was too young then to get the red scarf. When I reached the fourth grade, though, they gave it to me. This was another big thing for me at that time. It was the beginning of being recruited into the Communist Party. I don't think they do that anymore.

IV: My First Bra

The next big thing that happened was my mother going to a village to help the doctor there for six months. I got to stay with my father in Beijing. This was the most time I ever spent with my father while I was growing up.

He showed me the history of Beijing, and I learned a lot more about the history of China. He taught me to ice skate and swim. He taught me some martial arts and how to play Ping-Pong and tennis. I learned a lot of things from him.

At that time, my father was the head of all the athletes in China, including the Olympic athletes. When I stayed with him, I realized how talented and educated my father was. Before that I hadn't really known much about him at all. I also found out he was a great cook. We had so much fun cooking and eating together.

"Yanyan, why are you always standing like that?" my father asked one night while he was cooking something for us to eat.

I was at the age when my breasts were starting to develop. I was so uncomfortable and shy about it. I always had my arms crossed and my head down.

"I don't know. I just feel comfortable like this," I told him.

I was too shy to tell him why I was really standing that way. I was always scared and timid around my father.

"Is it because you're embarrassed about something?" he asked. "Because it looks like you're embarrassed about something."

"But I didn't do anything wrong," I assured him.

"I know you didn't do anything wrong," he said, "and you don't have anything to be embarrassed about, either."

Then he sat down in a chair and looked right at me. "That's the beauty of being a girl. You are growing," he told me. "You should never be shy about your body. You should always be proud of who you are."

Every time he saw me standing that way, he would make me stand with my heels, butt, shoulders, and head touching the wall for at least fifteen or twenty minutes. He found out that I was putting a piece of cloth across my breasts and tying it tightly in the back.

In China at that time, there was nowhere to get bras for little girls. It was hard enough for a woman to get one. He wrote a letter to my mother, telling her to make one for me out of one of hers.

When I was with my mother, she taught me all the things a girl should know, such as sewing, washing and folding clothes, and doing needle work. When I was with my father, it was completely different. He showed me all the things a boy should know, such as being aggressive and playing checkers, and he taught me more things about sports and the history of our country.

These are not all things that I think only a boy should know, but I was not used to them. He taught me a lot of martial arts and told me to never be afraid of anything. I found a new power inside myself when I was with my father in Beijing. He tried to teach me everything he could in the short time that I was with him. He finally had his daughter for more than fifteen days. He knew I would be going back to my mom soon. This was his chance, his one real chance, to be my father.

I did a lot of things for the first time when I was with my father in Beijing. He took me to a restaurant where they served only Peking Duck. We went to the Forbidden City and the Qing Dynasty Museum.

The underground palace is something I will never forget. There are so many statues; they just go on forever. They are still digging them up, as far as I know. I didn't know that they used to put living people in there until my father told me. That was really creepy. There are some terrible ways to die.

He told me that when an emperor who had treated the people badly would die, everyone in his family and everyone who had worked for him would be buried alive with him. This makes me think of their young wives—they always had the youngest wives. I feel terrible for all those people. I'm glad I didn't live back then. I remember getting chills when my father told me all that stuff. That's probably why he kept going, but I know he didn't make any of it up.

This was also the time when I took my first trip to a regular restroom. They were only in the big hotels or government buildings.

"There's something I have to show you," my father said one day with a smile and a wink.

I could tell it was going to be something exciting, but I had no idea how big and exciting. It was my first glimpse of the modern world. He took me to the building where he worked. "Go use the restroom, Yanyan," he told me.

I went into the restroom and immediately came right back out. "There's no hole there," I told him.

"It's a toilet. You see that tall white ceramic thing, with water in it? You can use that. When you're finished, I'll show you how to flush it."

I had no idea what he was talking about. I went inside and took a look at the thing. The first time I went in there, I'd been looking for a hole in the ground, and I hadn't even noticed this toilet thing he was talking about. I'm laughing so hard at this memory as I'm trying to write it.

I had no idea how to use a toilet. First, I stood there, just looking at it. I tried to stand up on it and squat down. It never dawned on me to sit on it.

"You have to sit down on it, Yanyan," I heard my father say from the hallway. "Be careful—don't hurt yourself."

He heard me fall down and knew what I was doing. When he came in and showed me how to flush it, I thought it was the most brilliant thing man had ever created.

This was one of the greatest experiences of my life, and going back to the holes in the ground was one of the worst. This was a bathroom, a restroom. The holes in the ground were not. They were a place where you did your business and got out.

The building where my father worked had a restroom. A place that had no bad smells. A place where you wanted to take a short rest, like the word *restroom* implies. The building had a bathroom. A place where you might take a moment to wash your face and hands, like the word *bathroom* implies. I had never seen a sink with running water or even a mirror in the restroom—only holes in the ground.

My father should have never shown me the restroom that day. It spoiled me. I never would have known how bad the holes really were. I used that restroom every time I got the chance while I was in Beijing. I would get my father to take me there sometimes, even when I didn't have to go.

My stay in Beijing was also the first time I saw foreigners. We went to the area where all the different embassies from around the world are located. He pointed out each individual flag and told me what country it represented. I had seen them only in pictures in my schoolbooks. Now I was watching them flying in the wind, in all their glory.

It was wild, too, to see foreign people walking around. I had never seen them, even in pictures. A tall black man walked up to us and said in Chinese, "Hello, sir. And how are you, little girl?" I thought I had lost my mind. My father started to laugh at my reaction as he told the man we were fine and having a wonderful day. When I saw a blonde woman with blue eyes, it was just too much. I might as well have been on a set for the movie *Star Wars*. At the time, I didn't even know what a movie was. The next day, my father took me to a planetarium. That blew my young, fragile mind right out of the water.

My father also took me to the Great Wall and showed me television for the first time in my life. Now I realize it was just Chinese news. In China, I think the government still runs all television to this day. But they do have variety shows and movies now. The whole entertainment field is bigger in China now. In fact, it's just like America, except there are no adult channels. When television first hit China, it wasn't seen as entertainment like it was in America. It was used by the government to speak to the people, as a propaganda machine. I'm not saying it hasn't been used for that in America, but in China, it wasn't seen as entertainment at all at first.

The craziest thing of all was when he took me to the Beijing zoo. I had never seen anything like it. They didn't have pictures of animals like that in my schoolbooks or anywhere else. I surely had never seen the real thing. In my town, all we had was basically a petting zoo, with chickens, goats, and animals like that. The Beijing zoo had elephants, tigers, zebras, and many other kinds of animals I had never seen. I kept asking my father if they were real. When my father told me to read the signs at each enclosure, I saw that the animals were from all over the world. It made me kind of sad to know they were all so far from their homes. I made my father take me to the zoo every weekend to visit those animals the whole time I was in Beijing.

I saw more cars than I had ever seen before, as well as traffic lights. Xinxiang had no traffic lights and very few paved roads when I was growing up. We even went to the Beijing opera, another first for me. I didn't understand one thing about it. It didn't matter, though; I was with my father in Beijing.

I didn't want to leave Beijing. I missed my mother, but Beijing is the capital of China. It's an incredible city. I loved the school there, being with my father, and everything about it. Eventually, though, I had to go back home to Xinxiang City.

When I returned home, I had changed so much. I didn't even speak the same way anymore. I spoke like they do in the big city. I had new confidence in myself. My mother knew it right away. She had made me a bra, and now I was proud of my breasts. I was the only girl in my whole school to have a bra, possibly in my whole city. I was the only girl around who had done a lot of things, at that point. My father was right: wearing that bra did make me feel more comfortable about my body. Everything about me changed really fast around that time. I guess I was growing up.

When I tried to tell my friends about the things I had seen in Beijing, they thought I was lying. "You're making it all up," they said. "There were no foreign people; those were monkeys."

"They have white monkeys too," an older boy said. "Some monkeys are as big as humans."

"No, they talked to me and my father," I told them. "They were people."

"Yeah, right—monkeys that speak too," one of my friends said. "You're just a liar."

Then they all laughed at me.

When I told them about the zoo, they said that the animals were fake.

"Do people in Beijing have wings?" one girl asked. "I've heard they have wings. That people there are taller than us, and they have wings."

"Yeah, and they also have three eyes," one boy said.

I couldn't believe they were saying those things and that they thought I would make it all up. When I told them about the toilet, even my best friend said, "I'm not going to be your friend anymore if you don't stop lying to us."

That's when I just gave up and said to myself, *My friends are stupid.* I know they were all just jealous and giving me a hard time.

I was the talk of the town. Everybody wanted to know about Beijing; no one had ever been there. They saw that I was dressing, talking, and acting differently. At my school, the teacher would always pick a student to stand at the front of the class and read a chapter from whatever book we were reading at the time. I had never gotten picked before. You have to stand up there, face everyone, and read loudly. I'd been too shy to do something like that, and my teacher knew it. Now she was picking me all the time, and I actually enjoyed it.

In school, different students would be chosen to announce the day's events over the loudspeakers. Never in my wildest dreams had I ever thought I would do that. But sure enough, one day the principal pointed at me and said, "You'll make the announcement today."

I will never forget it. I felt so special, like someone very important.

Everyone had always thought my mother and I were weak, because I was an only child and my father was never there. Plus, I was a girl. We had no other relatives living in Xinxiang. It was just me and my mother. No one ever saw us as weak after that.

Everyone had new respect for me. All the girls, even the older ones, wanted to see my bra. It used to be my doll; now it was my bra. They asked me where I'd gotten it, since they thought I'd lied to them about everything else. I told them my father had sent it from Beijing. They had never seen one that small, so they believed me.

Finally, my best friend, Xilin, said to me one day, "Yanyan, you were making those things up, right? Just to mess with everybody, right? I wasn't really mad at you. I knew what you were doing."

"No, I didn't make any of it up," I said. "It's all true."

"Even the part about the toilet?"

"Especially the part about the toilet."

I look back now and understand that we lived in a very small town. Most of my friends, even their parents, had never been anywhere or seen anything outside of our little town. No wonder they thought I was making it all up.

Xinxiang was a little town that became a big city; that's why my mother had been sent to work in the hospital there. It was a new hospital. A lot of new buildings were there. When I got my first bike, at about ten years old, they paved the road right in front of our complex; I couldn't believe it. All my friends had bikes, but they'd had such a hard time learning to ride them on the dirt road. I got to learn on the pavement. It wasn't as forgiving as the dirt, but it was much easier to learn to ride, and I didn't fall down nearly as much as the other kids did. I liked growing up in Xinxiang City, and I have a lot of good memories.

I used to collect things like pieces of glass, empty toothpaste tubes, pieces of metal, used books, and empty boxes, anything that could be recycled. Once a week, they would push a big cart through our complex. It was for recycling, and they would give you money right there. Every week

I was out there, waiting for the cart to come. They would ring a bell, and as soon as I heard it, I would get so excited. This was how I got money to buy candy, hair ribbons, pencils, erasers, or anything else I wanted that I knew my mother wouldn't have the money for.

Competition was stiff, though—I wasn't the only kid in the neighborhood who was recycling. There were even more adults with regular routes. It wasn't much money, but it always made me feel good when I bought something for myself.

I had always collected things. My favorite was candy wrappers. I used to trade them with other kids. When I came back from Beijing, I had a lot of new ones that no one had seen before. None of the boys had ever really noticed me, but now they all wanted to see my candy wrappers. Some of them started giving me candy wrappers and hanging around the water faucet outside our door. I guess it was because of my new bra. Plus, I had found a new confidence in myself.

One of the neighbors told my mother that her son never wanted to help her with anything. Now every day he wanted to know if she needed water, or if she needed vegetables washed, or anything that had to do with using water. She said she didn't understand, because he had never wanted to go get water before. He'd always said it was too far, and he would make his older brother go. Then his older brother told her the change had occurred when I had returned from Beijing. I'd always liked him, but I never knew he liked me. He proved his affection when he helped me with the caterpillars. I had some caterpillars in a jar, but I was running out of leaves to feed them. They ate a certain kind of leaf, and it was hard to find them. He brought me a whole box full. I have no idea how he got so many. He was the one who made me start thinking about boys.

I was always good at art. One of my favorite things to do was make pieces out of cut paper. I don't know if you have ever seen this. It's a picture cut from one continues piece of paper. I was really good at it. There is a name for it, but I can't remember it. My mother got me started on it, because I had no patience when I was little. I had the hardest time focusing or staying in one place at school.

"If you can take your time and get good at doing this," she told me, "then it will help you in school."

"How is making a picture going to help me with school?" I asked her.

"Because they tell me you can't focus on your schoolwork," she said. "If you learn to do this, you'll have more focus at school and more patience at home."

She turned out to be right. They say mother knows best. The craft helped me with my focus and taught me patience and discipline. Actually, it helped me with a lot of things. It's like a form of meditation. Who knew you could learn so much just from doing some art? I can't believe I became good at it. It's so difficult.

I told my mother in the beginning that I would never be able to do it. All I did was tear the paper up as soon as it started looking like something. Or I would cut it the wrong way, ruining the whole thing. It was so frustrating, and I realized my mom was right: I had no patience at all. I would get angry and throw the scissors and paper everywhere. I would stand up and scream and stomp in a circle. Sometimes my mom would laugh at me, but sometimes she would get as mad as I was. I was crazy as a child. I had all kinds of energy and nothing to do with it. In China at that time, there weren't many activities. I had no TV or radio. I had no brothers or sisters to play with.

The rainy days were the worst, and it rained a lot. My father wasn't there; it was just my mother and me; and my mother worked all the time. That's why it was so hard on me when I lost my baby doll, Niuniu. She was my main activity after school. I always had to rush home to take care of her. I was completely lost when she first went missing. My mother tried everything to get me past it.

Doing the cut paper was what finally did it, I think. I remember rushing home after school to work on some piece I had started when I was finally getting good at it. I entered one of my pieces in a school competition and won first place. My mother was so proud of me. She started hanging my art all around the house.

Just when I started feeling like I was finally fitting in and becoming popular, my mother and I moved from Xinxiang City back to Kaifeng. I was very sad and cried for many days. The day before we left, all my friends came. We took a lot of pictures, and they brought me cards and letters.

When we finally moved, I was lonely. I had to start all over again. I had to go to a new school and make new friends. I really missed my friend Xilin. I am an adult now, and I still talk to some of those friends from Xinxiang.

I was no longer in the girls' group I had been in at my other school. It wasn't that bad, though. Kaifeng is a very old, traditional city, with a lot of history. Plus, I have a lot of cousins who live there. It's the city where my mother and father grew up. It's where they met and got married, and it's the city I was born in. I spent the last year of elementary school there and all of middle school. I love Kaifeng.

With the newfound confidence I had from spending so much time with my father in Beijing, I managed to land myself a position at my new school. Each class assigned representatives for each subject. I was the representative for sports and entertainment. I was also the conductor for the choir in my class, and I led the exercise period each day.

I'd thought I was popular when I lived in Xinxiang, but now I had become really popular. All the boys started to like me. I was really shy and naive, still under my parents' wing. I am still naive about a lot of things, and sometimes I feel like I am still under my parents' wing.

V: The Red Money Bags

In the middle of February came the Chinese New Year. I used to love that time of year. Winter break started January 1 and lasted all the way to the end of February, giving us two months of vacation.

Normally I got all new clothes, including underwear, socks, and shoes. Everything would be new. I only got this once a year. All the mothers made new clothes for their children for the New Year. All the kids waited the whole year for this. In November and December, it was all we talked about.

Once the gifts had been given, it was like show time. All the kids would come out at almost the same time to show off their new clothes. It wasn't like anybody was wearing anything that fancy. It was more about seeing how much time and effort had been put into making your clothes. I never had to worry: my mother was very good at making clothes. She still is.

During the New Year's celebration, there was lots of food from morning till night, and no one slept—even the kids stayed up all night. We played cards and made a big bonfire. On the first day of the New Year, all the kids got up really early to say "Happy New Year!" to our parents and older relatives. They gave us a little red paper bag with some money in it.

I always felt bad about growing up an only child. Being a girl made it even worse.

In China, your family is almost considered a failure if you have no children or only one child, especially if that one child is a girl. It's like people think you must be from bad blood or your ancestors did something wrong and you're being punished for it. It doesn't really matter, though.

I was the only child in my family, and a girl, but our relatives never saw us that way.

Only outsiders and old, traditional Chinese people believe these things to be true. I think the reason is that China used to be all farmland. The more children you had, the stronger your family was. The more boys you had, the more land you received. Plus, boys stayed home. When they married, their wife moved in with the family. If you were a girl, you would be married off, and you would move in with your husband's family.

But during the New Year celebration, I didn't feel bad about being an only child at all. I was glad. I would find ten yuan in my red bag—more than I would have gotten if I'd had brothers and sisters. My cousins would get only two yuan because my aunts and uncles had four or five children. Even my paternal grandmother would give me eight or ten yuan instead of two.

"You're my favorite grandchild, even though you're a girl, and there's only one of you," she would tell me. "I believe you can do more than all my other grandchildren."

She always made me feel good about myself. I always felt strong and proud after talking to her.

"Don't let your cousins know I gave you that much money," she would say. "Don't lose it. And don't you let anybody cheat you out of it, either."

She always made me want to study harder and work harder. She made me want to try my best and help my parents and all my relatives.

I always felt like a little rich girl when the Chinese New Year came around. And that's just two red bags, one from my parents and one from my paternal grandmother.

Then I would see my maternal grandparents. In a Chinese family, all the grandchildren spend the first day of the New Year with their paternal grandparents, and the next day with their maternal grandparents. Then the family gathers at one another's houses, starting with the oldest uncle and going all the way through to the youngest aunt, including only the aunts and uncle who are married. Still, this can take weeks.

I just loved that time of year when I was growing up. So many parties, seeing all the friends and relatives together, all the gifts, the red money bags—it was all just great. It was the greatest thing about my childhood.

I miss New Year's in China a lot. New Year's happens all over the world, but not like in China—not for me, anyway. The Chinese New Year is something special.

When I went to my mother's parents' house, it was a little different. They were well established in the community and enjoyed a pretty good lifestyle. I'm not saying they were rich by any means; but, for example, they had a toilet near their house that they shared with only three other families, and you could lock the door for privacy. They also had running water in their kitchen. We had only the faucet outside the door at my house, and we shared with everyone, just as we shared the toilets. They had more room in their house and a bigger kitchen. Everything was just nicer at their house.

Nobody was rich in China at that time; everybody was equal. They did have everything they needed and then some, though. I would get one red bag from my grandfather and one from my grandmother. There would be twenty yuan in each bag. You know how much money that was for a little Chinese girl living in Communist China at that time? Damn, I was rich. When my mother's siblings started having children, I didn't get as much. I had to share it with my new cousins. But for a few years, I was the only one they were concerned with, and I was cleaning up. When I was ten years old, right after New Year's, my mother knew I had money. She asked me if she could have some until the first of the month. I felt like I was an adult. I had power for once in my life.

The only thing about going to see my mother's parents that bothered me was that my grandfather's mother was still alive. She didn't pass away until I was twenty-eight, when she was one hundred and eight. She was already old when I was a little girl. I remember her being so tiny and gray. All she did was sit in the same chair with the same clothes on all day, every day. When she did get up, she walked completely hunched over, which made her look even smaller. I hate to say it, because she was my great-grandmother, but I was scared of her. I don't think I ever spoke to her until I was fourteen or fifteen years old.

"Yanyan, come here," she would say. "I want to see you up close."

But I would always run or hide behind my mother. When I got older, I started talking to her, though. She was a really cool woman. By the time I realized how cool she was, she was gone.

"Great-Grandma, what's your name?" I yelled into her one good ear. I must have been about twenty.

"My name?" she asked. "My name is Mrs. Kong."

"No, what's your name?" I asked. "What's your first name?"

She paused for a minute, just looking at me. "I don't know. It's been too long," she finally said. "I can't remember."

In old China, when a woman got married, she pretty much lost her identity. Everyone called her by her husband's last name. My great-grandmother got married when she was twelve years old. That means she was almost one hundred years old when I asked her that question.

It's always made me sad to know she didn't even know her own name. But I've also always felt good about the fact that my grandfather was such a good son to her. He took care of her until she passed.

As I mentioned earlier, when we lived in Xinxiang, the water was right outside our door. I used to think it was a pain for everyone to always be coming to our door. There was always a crowd, especially in the mornings; I hated it. Every morning, before it was even time for me to get up for school, I would hear the same old man clearing his throat over and over. It used to drive me crazy.

Man, was I stupid! What a luxury it was to have the water right outside our door. I couldn't have had it any easier. Now that we had moved to Kaifeng, I had to go get water the same as everyone else. You know how far it was? I can tell you this: it was not right outside my door. Oh, no! It would take me usually about a half hour or forty-five minutes. On a bad day, when there was a big line—and there was always some kind of line—it could take me over an hour.

We had one of those big wooden poles with chains and hooks on each end to hold wooden baskets of water. It was really heavy. Even without water in the baskets, it was heavy. When the baskets were full of water, it was ridiculous. I was only around eleven years old at the time. In the beginning, my father showed me how to carry it without water.

"It's all about balance. Otherwise you'll spill the water," he kept telling me. "You'll fall down and spill the water, and you'll probably hurt yourself."

Every day after school, I had to carry those damn baskets around the house. It was like my homework. Then my father would take the whole thing with him and come back a little while later with the baskets full of water. I remember him being like a coach. He would tell me to bounce, and he would count, one, two, one, two. I remember it like it was yesterday. "It's all about the bounce, Yanyan, it's all about the bounce." I can hear him right now.

I even dreamed about carrying water with that thing. They were nightmares.

When I finally did start going to get the water, my father followed along with me, and we filled the pots only halfway at first. I started to realize what he meant about bounce and balance. It was really hard. I had to stop three or four times to rest on the trip back home.

I never made that trip with my father or alone without stopping at least once to rest. I didn't want to fetch water at all. It was mostly men or older boys getting the water. There might be an older woman or two there, but no one like me, that young and a girl.

Everyone had several children. I was an only child, and my father worked in another city. When I finally started carrying the water on my own, my shoulders were bruised and swollen. That was one of the worst jobs I ever had in my entire life. Sometimes I cried on the way home, because my shoulders were hurting so badly. When I complained to my mother about it, she would say, "You have to take the good with the bad. Remember how much you like New Year's? Your father comes home once a year to help you. Right now you have to do it by yourself." I know that my mother and father are the main reasons I am so disciplined in my life now.

We used to get water for free when we lived in Xinxiang, but in Kaifeng, we had to purchase the water. It wasn't much—only five cents for each pot. But that was a lot back then; every penny counted. Once when I was coming home, I bounced all wrong, lost my balance, and fell down.

You'll fall down, you'll spill the water, and you'll hurt yourself. I heard my father's voice in my head as I was going down.

I didn't get hurt, but the water went everywhere, just like my father had told me it would. It was more embarrassing than anything. My mom was so angry; she made a big deal about it. I felt so stupid. I never dropped the water again after that.

We had a big storage barrel for the water at our home. I was too little to dump the pots into the barrel. I had to get a cup and dip the water out until the pots were light enough so that I could pick them up and dump them in. Sometimes my older cousins would come and help me. That was a great relief.

I hated getting the water. That was the worst part about living in Kaifeng.

I became a role model for girls my age. Their mothers would point at me and say, "Why can't you be more like Yanyan? She doesn't mind doing the hard work."

Little did they know, I hated it. I did it only because I had no brothers or sisters and my father wasn't there.

33

Other people looked down on me. They thought something must be wrong with our family, and that was why I was getting the water. Everybody had more than one child at that time. Some people even thought I was adopted. I didn't know why some adults were mean to me, but later I found out that, in China, it's a bad thing to be adopted, because it means nobody wanted you. The people who adopted you would usually treat you badly and use you to do all the chores they didn't want to do.

I was confused for a long time, thinking my parents had been treating me badly, until I finally found out from my grandparents which hospital I was born in. I went there and discovered that my parents are mine and mine alone. Then I had a new attitude about things. I realized my parents really did care and really were trying to teach me. I understood how they wanted me to know everything before I grew into an adult.

Now I know that all those things made me stronger not only physically but also mentally. I became more disciplined, like I said. I can overcome almost anything. It made me a survivor. I can't put into words how much I appreciate the fact that my parents taught me about discipline, hard work, and common sense. These are things you can't learn in a book.

"Be glad we're poor," my father always told me. "When you're poor, you learn more about life, you grow up faster, and you grow up stronger." I think he was right. It makes you appreciate the good things you have in life.

When I was about thirteen, my father had a serious conversation with me.

"China is going to change soon, Yanyan," my father told me. "Don't feel bad because you're our only child, or because you're a girl."

"But I do feel bad. Some people think I'm adopted," I told him, starting to cry.

"Be strong, little girl. You're not adopted. In your lifetime, you will see things change so much." My father hugged me. "When you're an adult, China is going to be completely different. You'll see."

My father was right. Everything is completely different in China now. I watched it change right before my eyes as I grew up. It was because of my father's position in the government that he knew all those things. He wouldn't have been allowed to tell us, though. All he could do was hint at it.

In 1976, China was shaken to its core. In January, the first premier of China, Zhou Enlai, passed away. In July, one of the largest earthquakes in the world hit the city of Tangshan; over two hundred thousand people were killed. Later that same year, in September, Chairman Mao, the leader of China, died.

When the Tangshan earthquake happened, most of the doctors there lost their lives. All the hospitals were destroyed. They sent doctors from different provinces to help with the relief effort. My mother was sent, of course. She left me with my grandparents.

I can't remember how long it was. I know she was gone for months. When she came back, she was skin and bones. She was dark, because she had been out in the sun so much. She told me later that the only way they could get food was if it was flown in by plane or helicopter. She said that water was a real problem.

My mother told me years later that the reason she'd lost so much weight there was that she couldn't eat. She said she saw so many dead children that she had no appetite the whole time she was there.

When Chairman Mao died, the whole city mourned his death. I got really spooked, especially that night, after dark. There was such a gloomy feeling in the air. This was the beginning of another big change for China.

Once Mao had died, China went through the whole Hua Guofeng, Gang of Four, fiasco. A lot of change happened fast, but if you want to know about all that, read the history books. I was too young to understand most of it when it was happening. I know it made a lot of difference in the average Chinese person's life. The standard of living has gone way up in China since then.

When my father lived in Beijing, a lot of the money he made went toward travel expenses. Beijing is the capital of China, and it costs more to live there; everything is more expensive, as it is in New York City or Los Angeles. My father spent a lot of money on train tickets, traveling back and forth between Beijing and Xinxiang, and between Beijing and Kaifeng. Train tickets weren't cheap, and he always brought gifts. When he moved to Zhengzhou, he was able to save some money, so our situation started getting better.

Finally, my parents put up enough money to hire a plumber, and we had fresh running water in our home for the first time in my life. It was a glorious day for me. No more going to fetch water, no more old water from an old barrel. I looked down in that barrel once and saw that it was green at the bottom. I'm sure my parents were happy too—they didn't have to pay for water anymore. No more barrel! No more fetching water! No more fetching water!

Imagine the difference this made in a little girl's life. Water was no longer a fear or a worry for me. Water was free in my house. Wash my face? No problem. Have a drink? No problem. Water was no longer an issue.

VI: Uniforms

When my father made the move from Beijing to Zhengzhou, I started to see him more often, at least once a month in the beginning. Later on, it was even more often than that. Mostly he came to us, but sometimes my mother and I took the train to Zhengzhou to visit him.

My father's position was too high for him to be sent to run the sports facility in Kaifeng, where my mother and I were living. They sent him to Zhengzhou instead. At least it was much closer than Beijing.

I loved the trips on the train; they made me feel well traveled. The reason I was so popular at school was that most kids in China at that time, and even adults, didn't get to go anywhere. Traveling wasn't on the menu when you were just trying to make it through each day. Most people didn't have money for vacations.

I was twelve years old and had already lived in four different cities. One of them was the capital of China, Beijing; another was the oldest city in China, Kaifeng. I had also traveled to the farms and villages with my singing and dancing group. I guess I was well traveled. I had learned so much about life from my father in the six months I was with him in Beijing.

The trains in those days were very slow, not like the express trains they have today. They stopped at every little town and village for ten or fifteen minutes to load and unload passengers. Whenever I rode the train with my father, he made me get off at each stop with him.

"I want you to know what it really means to be poor," he would tell me.

He would point things out: the people living in makeshift houses; the children with no shoes and hardly any clothes; the starving dogs standing in the street, right beside kids who were as hungry as they were. I would see kids wearing shoes that were way too big for them, and I would think to myself, *At least they have shoes on their feet*; most kids I saw had no shoes on at all. They always looked so dirty, like they had never had a bath, and they were very skinny, like they never ate anything.

I would see them trying to sell water, boiled eggs, and other things so they could get some money. Sometimes when I got back home, I would think about those kids while I was lying in my bed, all warm and comfortable, and I would cry.

When I started to see my father more often, things changed a lot for me. I had always been into dancing, singing, and anything having to do with entertainment. Now my father got me into sports. Every day when he was home, he would wake me up in the morning to go running for one hour. Even when he wasn't around, he told my mother to make sure I went running every day. He told me that when they held tryouts for track and field at my school, I had to try out for the track team. I did, and I made the team.

First, I was the top runner in my school. Then I was the top runner in my city. Then I started playing basketball as well as running track. Then I became the top runner in our whole province. My father was the head coach for all athletes in Beijing. Now he was running the Olympic training facility in Zhengzhou. I didn't know it at the time, but now I see how he had arranged things for me. I'm not saying I wasn't good at playing basketball and running track. But I think he put a word in for me, since I was his daughter.

I was recruited from my school to relocate to Zhengzhou to try out to be one of the athletes who represent China. I was so excited; I knew if I could make the basketball or track team, I would be able to stay the whole summer with my father. My mother was excited for me, but she didn't want to see me go. I knew I was going to miss her, but at that point in my life, I was always missing either my mother or my father.

I kept thinking about how much fun I'd had with my father when I stayed with him in Beijing. Also, this was a chance for me to learn about a new city. I really liked what I had seen when my mother and I had visited my father there.

The reason they were recruiting so many young athletes from the schools around China was that they were trying to build a stronger record at the Olympics. For me, this was like winning the lottery. I had only just started playing sports the year before. I had to tell my cousins about it, all of whom were boys. I knew they would be so jealous.

"Let's just wait until you go for the tryout, Yanyan," my mother told me. "We don't want anyone thinking you're a failure if you don't get chosen."

"I have to be the one who tells them," I insisted.

I know she just didn't want me rubbing it in their faces. But I did go and tell them. All of them were upset.

"I'm a better athlete than you are," one of my cousins said. "Why would they choose you instead of me?"

"Because I'm a girl," I told him, "and they know girls are better."

All my cousins laughed at me, but I didn't care. I was the one going to Zhengzhou.

"You'll be back. They're never going to want you," my youngest cousin told me.

Then they all laughed again.

My father came for the weekend. Sunday evening, my father and I told my mother good-bye at the train station, and then we were on our way to Zhengzhou. I could tell my father was full of pride.

"You were my little baby bird, and now you're starting to fly," he told me. "It won't be easy. It's serious work, like being in the army."

"Yeah, but I'm strong now. I can handle it," I told him.

"Six o'clock in the morning, eight hours a day. This isn't a game, Yanyan," he said very sternly.

"But you'll be there with me, right?" I asked.

"No, no, no, little girl." My father started to laugh. "I'm the head of the facility. I won't be the one training you."

He started telling me again how serious it was. He told me how China was a proud country that needed to prove its strength at the Olympics. He started to tell me stories about famous Chinese athletes from the past. He also told me stories about successful people and the struggles they went through to get where they were.

I know now that my father was filled with hopes and dreams of me being a successful athlete. I'm sure as soon as he heard they were recruiting young athletes from all around China he submitted my name.

Even though he was my father and the head of the facility, he told me I would get no preferential treatment. After he finished scaring the hell out of me, he let me sit there and think about it all. He didn't say a word for several minutes. I thought to myself, *Is he mad at me, or is he just tired of talking?*

"It won't all be bad, though. You can eat all the food you want," he finally said. "They have food that you've never even seen before. More meat, different kinds of meat, bread, all kinds of breads. All the vegetables and fruits."

I looked at him and said, "Like New Year's?"

"And soups, and desserts." My father just kept going.

My father was right about everything he told me. It was like the military—really hard. They held tryouts for one week to determine who would go home and who would stay in Zhengzhou for three more months of training. Then they would send more people home, and there would be an additional three months of training. The ones remaining after that would go on to Beijing to train for the Olympic team. We were told all this before the tryouts started. It was as if they had given me a gold key. All I had to do was work hard and practice, and everything would fall into place. Man, was I mistaken.

I made it through the first tryouts and found myself two weeks into the three months of training. It was grueling, to say the least. I didn't see my father at all. We worked all day, and we slept all night. The training facility was completely isolated and located outside the city of Zhengzhou. He stayed in one part of the facility, and I stayed in another. It was like prison; nothing was around, no town, no village. Everything they needed was there. You were allowed to leave only on the weekends. Sometimes we would ride the bus to Zhengzhou.

It was a prison for athletes. Well, it wasn't really, but that's what it seemed like to me, as a child. The only thing good there was the food. They had everything my father had described and more. You could eat as much as you wanted. We would be so hungry from working out all day that we would stuff ourselves. We were also going to classes for school at the same time. It was a lot of hard work.

When I first passed the tryouts, we went home for a week before the training began. The Sunday evening we were to leave, my mother and I packed all my clothes and some personal things.

"She won't need any of this," my father said. "Everything will be provided for her."

"What about my clothes, socks, underwear?" I asked. "What am I going to do, wear the same thing every day?"

My father just laughed. I couldn't understand what he was talking about.

But he was right. They did have everything there. They even had special athletic uniforms made for everyone. They were all burgundy, with the words "Youth Olympic Training Center" written on the back. I didn't need any of the clothes my mother and I packed. All I was doing was training, eating, sleeping, and going to classes. Mainly training. Plus, I was so proud and honored to be wearing that uniform. When we went into town wearing the uniforms, people treated us with great respect.

My father and I made several trips back home to see my mother during the first three months. The first time, we were all ready to leave when my father looked at me and said, "Aren't you going to wear your uniform?"

"I'm tired of wearing the uniform," I told him.

I had on the pants and shirt I'd been wearing the first day we went there. I had been wearing the uniform all the time. I had washed and folded it and put it away for Monday, when we would return. Then I thought, *He's right; I have to show it to my cousins and friends.* It dawned on me that once again I had something that no one else had. Just like my baby doll, Niuniu; just like my bra; just like going to Beijing. Sure I was an only girl—and I was so glad to be that girl.

On the train, I realized why my father had wanted me to wear the uniform. He was showing me off to everyone, telling them how hard I had been working and how good I was at basketball.

When we got home, my mother called everyone to come to our house. My grandparents, aunts, uncles, and cousins came, of course. I was a big show-off, I have to say. I was probably totally obnoxious. I know I annoyed the hell out of my cousins. But I was proud of what I was doing, and certainly proud to have something to brag about to the boys. Man, I'm glad my father made me put that uniform back on.

I was lucky I got to go home at all. The only reason I did was that my father was there, and he was going home to see my mother. Most kids were by themselves. Their parents didn't have the money to come on the weekends.

As always, money was tight. Now my father had to buy two train tickets for us when he wanted to go home for the weekend. He hinted at going by himself, but he knew right away that there was no way I was going to let him leave me there. I made that very clear.

The first trip was no problem. The second trip was a little different. "I don't have enough money to get tickets for both of us," my father told me solemnly. "You'll have to stay behind this weekend."

"No way. It's bad enough when you're here," I shouted. "I don't want to stay here without you, and I want to see Mom."

"I don't know what to do," he told me. "I don't have enough money."

"I can hide in the restroom," I said.

"What restroom?" he asked. "You mean on the train?"

"Yes, on the train," I said. "No one will know."

"No, Yanyan, we can't do that," my father said sternly. "You'll get caught for sure."

We argued about it for a while, but I won. I made it clear once again that he was not leaving me behind.

Hiding in the restroom worked like a charm. No problem. My father was sweating bullets, though. He just knew we were going to get caught.

Then my father got his own uniform. My uncle worked on the trains, and my father got him to send a train conductor's uniform in the mail. I thought it was the neatest thing in the world. My father was king in my eyes. He could do anything.

Later on, he even got one of those lights that the conductors carry. We were still bold, though. To save money, I still tried hiding in the restroom, since it had worked before. It worked two more times. On the third time, I was caught. As a consequence, we were charged more money than it would have cost for both of our tickets.

VII: Road Trips with Dad

My father finally decided to buy a moped. He called it a motorcycle, but it was a moped. We were both really happy; now our trips home could be on our own time. No more stopping at every town and village to load and unload. No more riding the bus to the train station from the sports facility. "This should knock a lot of time off the trip," my father told me. "We'll have more time to spend at home with your mother." Of course, it didn't work out that way. It's funny how life hardly ever goes as planned.

At first, the moped was great, although my father always had the hardest time getting it started. Plus, it leaked oil, and there are hardly any gas stations in China. As a matter of fact, I don't know where he got the gas. As I'm writing this, I'm thinking I'm going to have to ask him. I don't remember ever once pulling up to a gas pump. Every drop of gas I ever saw go into that moped came from a gas can. I never went with my father to fill the gas can, and I really have no idea where he got it. I wouldn't be surprised if he'd had a way of stealing it or even making it. I remember getting oil once from a military truck, but never gas.

We used to leave my house in Kaifeng at about three in the morning on a Monday so that we could be back in time for my father to go to work and for me to start my grueling day of training. I would be half asleep, so my mother would literally tie me to my father on the back of the moped. It was nice; snuggled up tightly against my father's back, I would just go back to sleep.

One time, it was still dark about two hours after we'd gotten on the road. I woke up when the moped stopped running. "What happened, Dad?" I asked.

"We're in for it now. The motorcycle is out of oil," he said. "Now I have to pedal, and we're going to be late." This was in the seventies, in Communist China; there were no cell phones, and no pay phones. There was no traffic on the road at all. It was pitch black, with no street lights or lights of any kind.

My father must have pedaled for several miles before we finally saw the lights of a military truck. He waved the truck down, and they gave us just enough oil to get to the next town. My father checked his watch every two minutes, certain we were going to be late. We actually got there about half an hour early. All his worrying had been for nothing.

Another time, the moped broke down right outside a small village. Daylight had just appeared. I was awake when the moped stopped running. My father cursed. Forgetting that I was tied to his back, he tried to get off the moped to see what was wrong, and we both fell over, along with the moped. That made him even angrier. He picked the moped back up and started pushing it, with me following along. Finally, we saw a farmer with a three-wheeled, motorized cart, and a pig running along behind it.

"Could you give us a ride to the next town?" my father asked. "This thing's not running."

"Yes, but hurry. My pig is sick," the old man said. "I've got to get him to town as quickly as possible."

My father put the moped in the bed of the old man's cart, and we climbed aboard. There was hardly any room, and it smelled really bad. The old man was driving so fast. It reminded me of when I was in that truck accident with my aunt. I just hung onto the moped and thought, *The poor pig is going to be dead before he gets to town.*

The pig was running behind the cart as fast as it could, grunting and squealing. Drool was running out of its mouth. I told you before, I'm not making any of this up. This is my life.

"What do you do for a living?" the old man loudly asked over the sound of the motor. "Where are you coming from?"

My family has always tried to dress well for travel. The old man knew we weren't from around there.

"I work for the sports facility in Henan Province," my father yelled from the back of the cart. "We're headed back there, coming from Kaifeng."

"No problem. I'm going to Zhongmu," the old man said when he heard this. "I can drop you at the local sports center in town."

I know in America nobody cares what your position is, but in China, if you have a position in any kind of official capacity, people always go out of their way to help you. I'm sure my father knew this. He told the old man that would be fine. When we arrived—I'm not kidding—there were about twenty people running around, doing everything they could do until that moped was running again. When it finally did start running, all those men were dancing, laughing, and singing. I was just a little girl, but I thought it was all really stupid.

I wasn't in a big hurry to get back to training, but my father didn't think it was funny. "We're going to be late, Yanyan. I'm sure we're going to be late this time."

But we weren't late; we got there on time. My father is never late. When I was a child, he always made sure he had plenty of time to get wherever he was going, and he's still that way. That's one thing I wish I could have learned from my father. I'm not like that at all. I'm not late all the time, but I do wait until the last minute to get everything together.

The first three months of training came to an end. The big day arrived when they would announce who would be going home and who would be staying for another three months of training.

When I first arrived in Zhengzhou for the initial tryouts, I thought there was no way I'd get chosen. Kids were there from all over Henan Province. Most of them had been playing sports for years. Now I knew for sure I would be going home. That was fine with me; I'd had enough of training camp. I had scars on my shins from jumping up and down on a Ping-Pong table so many times; I just couldn't make it again. The inevitable happened: both my shins hit the side of the table, and I went straight over on my face. I had blood running down both of my legs.

I couldn't cry in the gym, in front of everybody.

We were required to jump up and down on the Ping-Pong tables one hundred times each—three sets of one hundred. That was after, before, and in the middle of an obstacle course involving monkey bars, stretch exercises, push-ups, and several other things. See why my shins hit the table?

My father had told me in the beginning that I would receive no special treatment just because I was his daughter. But I did receive special treatment, and I think it was just because I was his daughter. No matter how hard I tried, or how well I did, I would always be asked to do more. And I mean more than they were asking anybody else to do. I got so good at shooting baskets, because they made me do it for hours. I'd really had enough of training camp.

On the day of the announcements, we faced more challenges. Each sport had different challenges. They thought I was too short for the basketball team, so my big challenge was to shoot one hundred baskets in a row. I had other things to do, but all of it was easy for me.

I made ninety-seven of my one hundred. My father gave me the same look of disappointment he'd given me when I dropped the pan of chicken feed. He told my mother that I'd missed on purpose, because I wanted to go home. I don't know what happened. In practice, I would always make the one hundred baskets.

"I would never tell your father," my mother said to me later on. "You can tell me the truth."

The truth is, I don't really know. I know I wanted to go home, and I was missing my mother. And I know for sure I was tired of training. But I also know I tried my best to make every one of those shots. I was happy inside, thinking I had done my best and that there was nothing else I could do. Now I would be going back home.

I didn't show my father that I was happy. And I didn't act happy when they announced my name, saying I had been chosen for three more months of training. You read that right. I was about to go through three more glorious, fantastic, beautiful months of sports training.

The second or third time we went home for the weekend, my mother told me, "You've gained weight, and you're looking so healthy."

"Of course, Mom," I told her. "All I do now is work out and eat."

I had gained weight. I was eating all the time. It wasn't fat, though; it was muscle. I was getting big and tall. My mother made me stand against the wall and made a mark right at the top of my head.

"Next time you're here," she said, "we'll see how much you've really grown."

Every time my father and I went home, I stood there and let her make a new mark on the wall. My parents were hoping and praying that I would get taller so I would be chosen for the basketball team.

The day of the announcements was very emotional and moving. Some of those kids were the only hope their families had for a better future. When they were told they would have to go back home, it was devastating for them. It was like one huge funeral where all the people there were close relatives of the deceased. They were all crying and moaning.

At the same time, you had all the people who knew they would be staying, so there was a huge celebration, with everyone so happy to be there. I just stood in the middle of it all, confused. I couldn't figure out why they'd chosen me for three more months of training. I hated seeing some of them leave. I had made some good friends, and we were all working very hard. To me, no one deserved to be sent home. Except me, of course. I wanted to go home.

I did work hard, as hard as I could. Now that I am older, though, I see that I didn't really respect the opportunity that was in front of me. The first three months of training had been so hard. I really don't know how I made it through the initial tryouts. So many kids were sent home that day, and I thought I would be leaving with them.

Later that night, I thought about some of the people I thought deserved to be there a lot more than I did. They wanted it more, and it was their only hope for the future. I don't think my dad really believed I would make it all the way to Beijing and ultimately the Olympics. I doubt he ever entertained the fantasy of me actually winning a gold medal. I think, more than anything, he wanted me to have access to all that good food while I was young and still growing. Plus, my mother had me spoiled. He wanted me to be in a situation where everything would depend on me and my attitude, where I would have to learn independence, responsibility, and social skills. Since I was the only girl in my family, even my cousins were always looking out for me. Now even my father wasn't looking out for me. I was on my own.

When I first arrived there, every night for at least a week, I cried in my bunk. I didn't want the other girls to know, but I couldn't help myself. I wanted to go home so badly, and I was missing my mother. That's how I would drift off to sleep every night in the beginning. I didn't realize it then, but there were a lot of girls like me, as well as boys. I'm sure everybody there missed their families, but some of those kids really were true athletes.

Once the next three months started, it got a little easier. My mother was upset because she wanted me back home, but she was also excited. She might have actually fantasized about me winning a gold medal. She was so proud of her daughter. She missed me, but she was hopeful for me.

The training didn't get any easier; it actually got harder. Staying there did get easier, however, and my social life picked up. I had a couple of new girlfriends with whom I had a lot of fun. We played games and told one another stories about growing up. We were all from different parts of Henan Province. I also had a new admirer—a boy named Dabing.

We had the same hot-water containers with the cork lids that my mother had had when I was little. When I took mine to get hot water one day, the lid popped off and fell to the floor. I don't know what happened to me. I'm such a fragile little thing sometimes, and I guess I was missing my mom. I know I was exhausted from all the training. I just started thinking about how I had never found my mother's lid and that I was probably going to fail at this training too. I started crying loudly, thinking no one was around.

"Are you all right? Do you need any help?" I heard a male voice say behind me.

Dabing picked up the lid and handed it to me. Every time I turned around from then on, he was there. Every time I found myself feeling down, like I wasn't going to be able to go on, he would be there to encourage me. I was so naïve; I thought he was just a nice boy, a good friend. He was a tennis player, and he also played guitar. Eventually, he played tennis at the Olympics. I became close to him and started to depend on him. But the very next time we found ourselves alone, he tried to touch me inappropriately. I was so disappointed and hurt. I really just needed a good friend. I was only thirteen at the time; he was older. Men—what can you do?

When the second three months of training came to an end, I thought I might actually have a chance of going to Beijing. I had become quite an athlete. I wouldn't call it excitement, though; I still wanted to go home. I was indifferent about the whole thing. But I knew I was a better person than before. All that training had changed me for the better. I had learned so much about myself and had improved my ability to communicate my feelings to others. Not only had I become physically stronger, but I was much stronger mentally. I had learned how to put myself in other people's shoes.

I had been mainly by myself throughout my life, and the only time there was unity in my surroundings was at school. Now I knew all about the importance of teamwork, being part of a team, and relying on your teammates. I learned a whole lot about trust and the meaning of true friendship. I still talk with some people from the training camp.

I stood and listened to all the names being called for the people who would be going on to Beijing. My mind was drifting; I thought about the time when my mother and I lived in Xinxiang. Then I started trying to think of the first New Year's celebration I could remember. How old was I?

"Did they call your name?" my friend Yaoxin asked as she came rushing up. "They didn't call mine."

That's when I realized no more names were coming across the loudspeaker. My name had not been called. I would not be going to Beijing. But I would be going back home to my mom. I almost got excited and wanted to tell Yaoxin I was happy my name wasn't called. But I saw my father walking our way. I tried my best to look disappointed.

"It's all right. I know you did your best. At least you were here with me for a while," my father said as he approached. "And I know you learned a lot from the experience. Plus, you got to eat all that great food."

I was surprised. I'd thought he was going to be much more disappointed. He seemed to be more disappointed about the fact that I would be going back home than he was about me not being chosen for Beijing. I know he had gotten used to seeing me daily. Now it would be back to seeing me once every few weeks. Nonetheless, I thought he was going to say that I had failed.

Ultimately, sports weren't my passion, but the training camp made me much stronger and more aggressive. After being on the basketball team, I wasn't quiet or shy anymore. We went to so many places and played so many teams. I really enjoyed traveling to the different cities.

I didn't even tell you about any of that. In a nutshell, the different teams from the training facility had to play other teams from other provinces. But that's all ancient history now. I'm not going back there.

When the time came for me to go to college, I got into the best school in my area, because I had been on the basketball youth team that represented Henan Province. Later on, after college, I got a job in import/export in one of the top companies in China, just because I'd been on the basketball team.

Once the initial shock of the announcements had passed, everyone started mingling and talking. Then a man came out and asked for everyone's attention. He proceeded to give a speech thanking all of us for participating. He said we were all very special athletes. His words were really moving and inspiring. It was Friday evening, and as soon as he was done speaking, my father said, "Get your things together. We're leaving for home soon." Then he told me, "I have a surprise for your mother too."

"What is it?" I asked.

"I'll show you when we're ready to leave."

I rushed off to get my things. I had been so proud of the uniform. Now I couldn't wait to get it off. The first thing I did was put on my regular clothes. It was like a job completed, and I never put that sports uniform on again.

I was waiting for my father by the moped when he showed up with a big bag that had a shoulder strap. "This is for your mother," he said. "You have to carry it too."

I already had my bag over one shoulder, and now he wanted me to carry this big bag over my other shoulder. I looked inside the bag—it was full of food. My father had packed a little bit of everything in there. There were desserts, vegetables, and a lot of meat. He'd even put in pieces of sliced watermelon. I knew my mother was going to be so happy. He had strawberries in there, too, something we hardly ever got.

It was hard carrying those two bags all the way back to Kaifeng on the back of that moped. But every time it got heavy, I just remembered it was for my mother. It was always heavy enough just carrying my bag. Luckily, my dad would strap his to the handlebars. If he'd had two bags, he probably would have tied one to my back.

I always had a good time going back and forth with my father from Kaifeng to the training facility. It didn't matter if we were traveling by train, or on the moped. But this time, it seemed like my father was celebrating with me the fact that I was going home. We sang loudly as we flew down the road. He would sing something to me, I would sing something to him, and then we would both sing together. He kept telling me jokes. He had me laughing so hard at one point that I almost fell off the back of the moped, trying to hold those two bags. We had a great time.

When we got home, my mother was so happy to see us. She took the food my father had brought and started making dinner for us. "This is just perfect," she said when she saw the strawberries. "I'm going to make a strawberry pie for your return home, Yanyan."

That night, I heard my parents talking when they thought I was sleeping.

"It all worked out perfectly. I had no idea she'd make it through the second tryouts," my father said. "I wasn't sure she could make it through the first. But I know she's better for going there."

"I'm so proud of her," I heard my mother say. "I can see she's stronger than ever."

It felt so good knowing I hadn't let my parents down. I'd thought I was my father's biggest disappointment in life when I missed those last three baskets. He was right, though; their plan did go perfectly. More than perfectly. Even though I knew I had been tricked, it was too late. The knowledge was already in my head. When my father left early Monday morning, it hit me that now I was going to be missing him again.

On his way back to Zhengzhou, the moped stopped running, for good this time. No matter, though; my father wasn't late. He called my mother at the hospital and told her he wouldn't be home for a while. He said he was going to save the money for a bicycle. That way he wouldn't need gas and oil but could still be on his own time and save the train fare.

Writing these things makes me think about a lot of stuff, such as the fact that we had no phone in our house. My mother and father could talk on the phone only because there was one at the hospital and one at the sports training facility. Nobody had phones in their houses.

So, writing this, I realize that if my mother hadn't been a doctor, working at the hospital, the only way we would have been able to hear from my father would have been through the mail. I remember when some families had an emergency, they sent messages through a teletype office. But there was a charge. We were really lucky. I'm realizing it more all the time.

My father finally bought a bicycle. He made his trips home on it for the next three years. It's about 65 miles from Zhengzhou to Kaifeng. Once he did it so fast that he broke the world record for speed. No one was there to document it. No one was there to celebrate except my father, my mother, and I, but we sure celebrated.

The next time he came home from Zhengzhou, he brought a radio, the first radio we ever had in our house. We'd had a small portable radio you could hang around your neck when I was six years old, but I broke it so fast that it doesn't really count.

The only time I'd ever heard music was when they played it through the loudspeakers at school or when I heard it from my mother's hospital, which was right across the street from our house. (In China, you live right near your work. Everybody does, or they used to before free trade.) Oh, and there were the boy who played violin and the girl who played the Chinese harp, and the rooster we had—he was a pretty good singer. But they played music only at certain times from the hospital. It wasn't like they had a request line, either. You were completely at their mercy.

When my mother and I moved to Kaifeng, my grandparents gave her a housewarming gift. It was a small grapevine in a pot. We planted it in front of our house. Later, it got big. One summer, it had grapes all over it. Everybody started coming and taking them. At first my mother was mad, but it didn't matter. There were so many grapes that even though people took a lot of them, we still had grapes all summer long.

Every day after school, I filled several pots for my cousins to take back to their houses. They lived on the other side of Kaifeng. I always liked that job. I knew whatever grapes I picked were going to be eaten by my family. You couldn't get fresh grapes just anywhere. But you know how grapes are—the next summer, there were hardly any.

✶✶✶

Here is a poem that my father and I wrote together on one of our road trips. It's loosely translated into English.

Coming Home

Coming home through the windy nighttime snow

New Year's is the coldest time to ride your bike in China

I hear the dogs bark and the roosters crow

My burden is heavy, don't you know

But as I make my way through the snow

My heart is like an arrow

Headed home …

Coming home through the windy nighttime snow

Covered with snow and ice from my toes to my head

Even my cheeks are rosy red

Icicles forming on my mustache and beard

But when the door swings open she'll know that I'm here

The family is happy together again

It seems like forever how long has it been

风雪夜归人

岁暮年关近，天寒送肉面。

疾步闻犬吠，负重归如箭

风雪夜归人、冰雪甲满身

闻声急启扉，妻女皆笑颜。

VIII: Arranged Marriages

Let me tell you about my heritage. My father's last name is Yang, belonging to the Yangjiajian family. The Yangjiajian family is known in China for twenty-seven generations of consistent loyalty to the state. My father's father was from Mongolia. He was an instructor for the army, training the cavalry on horseback. After he retired from the army, he came to Kaifeng, looking for a wife. When he saw my grandmother, he knew she was the one. He was much older than she was—she was fifteen.

Her parents wanted her to marry someone with money and someone closer to her age. But my grandfather was smart. He was a fortune teller and an herbalist, so he rented the nicest temple in Kaifeng and set up shop there. He had clients coming in every day from everywhere. My grandmother's parents were very impressed, so they allowed him to marry their daughter. They eventually had three boys and one girl. My father was the third in line, born on June 9, 1940.

My mother's last name is Kong, from the Kongzi family tree, which leads back seventy-four generations to Confucius. My mother's parents were the product of a completely traditional, arranged Chinese marriage. When they got engaged, they had never even seen each other. In arranged marriages, the bride would wear a big red piece of cloth over her head so that she could not see the groom and he could not see her. When the ceremony was complete, the groom could then remove the cloth from his new wife's head, as I mentioned before.

The day my mother's parents were married, when my grandfather went to remove the red cloth from my grandmother's head, a Japanese bomb hit the building they were in. China was at war with Japan. Everyone had to run for a bomb shelter. My grandfather and grandmother still did not know whom they were married to.

Later, when they found out, they realized they had met in the bomb shelter and had not particularly liked each other. They eventually had three girls and one boy. My mother was the first. She was born on November 14, 1939. They were married until they passed.

I had a great relationship with my grandparents when I was growing up, but I never got the chance to meet my father's father; he died before I was born. My father's mother was forty years old at the time, she never remarried. I've seen my father's father in only one picture, and it is a drawing. I think he was very handsome. He looked like Genghis Khan.

I asked my grandmother once why she didn't have any photos of him. She told me that back then it was expensive to get a photo made. My grandmother finally passed away when she was ninety-nine.

My marriage wasn't prearranged, exactly, but it was a little. My mother had a friend she'd gone to school with. They had stayed in contact through the years. Her name is Xiuhua, she had two sons and one daughter. My mother had me, of course. Each year she would send my mother pictures of her children, and my mother would send her a picture of me. When we moved from Xinxiang to Kaifeng and the Chinese New Year came around, our family was invited to her home for dinner. This is where I met her oldest son, my future husband.

His name is Lu. This happened just before I turned fourteen. He is one year older than I am. It was ironic: we had been looking at pictures of each other our whole lives. So it wasn't exactly prearranged, but our parents knew we liked each other right away. The first time I saw him, my heart started racing, and my face turned red. I could tell he was feeling the same way. It took us a long time to get together, though; we were both shy and inexperienced.

I didn't see him after that first meeting until about four months later. His mother sent him to our house with some eggs. When he found out I was the only one home, he got embarrassed and didn't know what to do with himself.

The first time we met, we didn't even speak to each other; all we did was say hi. But we kept staring at each other. Now I know what all the adults kept giggling about. This time we actually talked, but only for a minute, and then he was gone.

Some people still use the Mei Puo in China, but it is a dying tradition. None of my friends or classmates went through any of that. None of them had arranged marriages. I'm sure they probably still have arranged marriages in a lot of the rural areas, though.

An entire year went by before I saw Lu again. My grandmother had a party to which all the family friends were invited, including his family. This time we talked a little more. He told me he was going to college soon. I thought I wouldn't see him for a while, maybe never again.

By the time I was sixteen, Deng Xiaoping had become China's new leader, ushering in the beginning of the socialist market economy and free trade. It was also the beginning of me learning to speak English. All the schools across China started teaching English. Before that, no language curriculum was offered. Now that I am older, I look back and know it was because of free trade that all of that started. A lot of things changed. New policies were put in place. Living conditions improved greatly. We actually got our first refrigerator and TV around that time. They had even phased out food coupons by then.

My mother and I moved to Zhengzhou so we could be with my father. My family was finally together, for the first time in my life. But I hated it. I didn't know anyone there; it was a completely new city. Everywhere we had lived before, we had friends and family, except when I stayed with my father in Beijing—but I was in Beijing, so I was too excited to be bored or scared or lonely.

Now I missed everything about living in Kaifeng. It was my first year of high school. I joined the basketball team and started to make friends. Then my mother told me we had a guest coming from Kaifeng. I couldn't believe that it turned out to be Lu. He was going to be attending the university in Zhengzhou. When I found out, I was really excited, but I tried not to show it.

Later, he would find reasons to come by my house. First it was once a month, then it was once a week, and finally it was every other day. He would want to use our bicycle pump, or he would ask my father for tickets to a sporting event, or he would have some books for me to read. I started treating him like a big brother or other family member. I wasn't sure how he felt about me, and I wasn't sure how I felt about him. He started helping me with my schoolwork. Then he just stopped coming by.

"Do you think Lu is sick?" I asked my mother. "Have you talked to his mother?"

"Why?" she asked. "Are you worried about Lu?"

"I'm not worried about him," I said. "I just don't understand why he hasn't stopped by."

"Do you miss him?" my mother asked.

I was shocked. I realized I was missing him, and I was also worried about him. That's when I knew how I felt about him. All at once, I was scared. Before this, I didn't really care how he felt about me; now it mattered.

When friends had asked me who Lu was, I told them he was my cousin from Kaifeng. I don't know why I told them that; it just felt right at the time. One day, I was walking home from school with my friend Cuihong when she said she saw my cousin by the library. We went over to talk to him. Cuihong asked him why he'd come to the library near our school, when there was a library at the university. He said they had more books at our library.

I asked him why he hadn't stopped by my house; it had been three weeks. He said he'd been busy, and then he told me not to tell my mother I'd seen him. I thought this was strange, so I asked him why. He told me he'd come by when I was not there, but my mother was. My mother told him I was about to graduate from high school and needed to start studying for college, and that I didn't have time for boys. I got really angry, but he told me my mother was right—I did need to concentrate on my studies. College is so hard in China. It's hard enough just to get enrolled.

I knew he was right, but I still didn't like him siding with my mother. I realized he was at this library because he wanted to see me. I also realized that I shouldn't have told my friends he was my cousin. I got very jealous when he was talking to Cuihong.

When I was in high school, I was very popular, because I was at the top of the track team and was one of the best shooters on the basketball team. A lot of boys wanted to date me. They sent me poems and love letters. When I showed them to Lu, he got upset. He acted like an older brother, telling me how hard the tests were for college and that I should concentrate only on school.

Finally, he was at my house one day, and my mother asked him to help her with something outside. His book bag was lying on the table, and I could see a diary on top. I couldn't help it; I had to look inside. I couldn't believe what I saw. He'd written about why he was so upset that I was getting love letters from other boys. He'd also written a poem about how he missed me. There was one whole page of my name written over and over. Then I saw another line he wrote: "I think I love this girl." I got really excited, because I felt the same way about him.

I had a problem, though. One of my girlfriends had started asking me questions like "How has your cousin been doing lately?" and "Do you know where Lu is going to college?" I had to put an end to this, and fast. I needed to let them know he wasn't my cousin. He was my guy.

When I told them, they got the biggest kick out of it. "Oh, you've been trying to fool us all this time," they said.

"I always knew he wasn't your cousin," one of my girlfriends said. "I could tell by the way you look at each other."

Then we all laughed.

"Every time I see him, he asks me about you," another one said.

Now the cat was out of the bag.

We had to sneak around a lot. I'm not talking about sex—that was out of the question. I'm talking about the rule that said when you're in high school, you cannot have a boyfriend, girlfriend, or any other type of relationship, except with your parents.

I wasn't the only one who had a boyfriend or girlfriend. But the consequences of getting caught were severe. First of all, you would be kicked out of school altogether. Second, you would be looked at as a bad child. Third, and the worst of all, you would be a disappointment to your family. This is something, even to this day, that you just do not want to do in China, or anywhere else in the world, really.

In America, when you turn eighteen, your record pretty much starts over. No one is allowed to look at or bring up anything about your juvenile record. In China, it's not like that at all. Your record from the day you were born follows you for the rest of your life. That means that if you make a mistake as a child, it could ruin you for the rest of your life. And it could be something as small as having a boyfriend.

It goes further than that. Sometimes, something your ancestors did can follow you and your family's name, kind of like the Hatfields and McCoys. This has to be something really big, though, usually political.

Lu told me that even though the school year was ending and he had no money, he was not going home. He said that one way or another, he was going to stay for the summer in Zhengzhou. This made me very happy, because my parents would be leaving for two weeks. My grandmother was coming to stay with me, and she knew nothing about him being around.

He told his parents he was on the soccer team and wanted to stay for summer practice. But they knew it was because of me. That summer, we became a lot closer. I don't know how he did it. I don't know where he stayed at night or how he got any money. All I know is that we were together almost every day. This was the first time we actually went out together. We rode our bikes to the mountains, which took a full day. We left early in the morning and came back when it was almost dark. We didn't have any money, so we took some boiled eggs and canteens full of water. It wasn't nearly enough. I was so hungry, and we ran out of water, but I didn't care. I was having a great time.

My grandmother thought I was at my girlfriend's house. I was so innocent; I felt scandalous. That summer was the first time we'd ever kissed. It didn't come easily, and it didn't happen often. We were both shy and inexperienced, and there were always people around us. My mother and father watched like hawks when they got back to town. They thought Lu had gone back home when school ended. I was so happy when I told them he was going to stay. My father was a little upset.

I see now that he knew I was growing up and there was nothing he could do about it. Several fathers came around during that time, asking him if their sons could date his daughter. He would always tell them, "No, my daughter is too young. She's still in high school."

My mother would tell me whose father had come by and then ask me, "Do you like that boy?" My father never told me that anybody came by.

Lu's mother came to Zhengzhou to see what he was up to. She stayed at our house, of course. When she arrived, I served her and my mother tea while they talked and caught up.

Finally, she asked my mother if she'd seen Lu. I got so embarrassed. "It's a wonder he's not right here now," my mother said. "Every time you see Yanyan, you see Lu. And every time you see Lu, you see Yanyan."

His mother looked at me and asked, "Have you seen Lu?"

"Yes, I saw him yesterday," I told her.

"What has he been doing?" she asked with a smile.

"Practicing soccer and studying," I told her. "That's all he does, all the time."

She could tell by the way I said it that I thought he wasn't spending enough time with me.

By the time I was in my first year of college, everyone knew that Lu and I were an item, including the families.

Deng Xiaoping had changed so many things in China by then. This was why my mother and father were finally living together. During Mao's time, everything was done to make the country strong, but it tore a lot of families apart. Now everything was changing, and some of those families had the chance to reunite, including mine.

So many things have changed in China in my lifetime. By the time I was married, you were allowed to have only one child, and that was only if you and your husband's years on this planet added up to fifty years or more, combined. At the end of Mao's time, while the cultural revolution was happening, there was no college. All the graduating high school students from the cities had to go live in the villages and farms for a certain amount of time to learn how to farm and work; this was mandatory.

I just missed this, but I have an aunt just a few years older than me, who lived in a village for three years. My father sent me to stay with her for the whole summer break one year. I think I was eleven or twelve. Every day we had to get up early in the morning and work in the fields all day. I hated it; I had blisters all over my hands. My body ached every day. Looking back, I think it was good for me. Sometimes you should be taken out of your comfort zone. Otherwise you start to take things for granted.

By the end of my second year of college, China was starting to open its doors to the world. This was the beginning of talk about free trade. The government started pulling students from colleges around the country and placing them on new projects that were being developed. I was sent to a new oil refinery to teach the children of the workers there.

When I got on the bus to leave Zhengzhou, Lu was on his bike. I was crying, looking out the back window of the bus. He was crying and riding his bike behind the bus. He must have followed us for ten miles or more. Slowly but surely, he drifted farther behind. I finally saw him standing in the middle of the road, waving good-bye, and I didn't see him again for six months.

This is one of my worst memories. That picture of him in the middle of the road, waving good-bye, has never left my mind. I can see it as clearly today as I could then. I was so lonely, and I stayed on that job for two years. I saw him only twice a year while I was there, but I received a letter from him every other day. I still have those letters. Now I know what my parents went through all those years.

I missed him and my family so much. Then I found out from my aunt that a position in my city at an import/export company was available—they needed English speakers. I knew that since it was dealing with imports/exports it was more important than the job I was doing at the oil refinery. My English wasn't that good, but I decided to apply for the job, and it turned out they wanted me right away.

It wasn't easy to get my file transferred from the oil refinery to the import/export company. My mother decided she'd pretend to be ill. Since I was an only child, I would need to be close to home to take care of her.

This job was perfect for me. Now I could be with my family again and near Lu. Remember, as I said earlier, what finally sealed the deal was the fact that I'd been part of the youth basketball team in Henan Province.

So I started my new job, and, not long afterward, I found out I was pregnant. I was so happy; I wanted to have Lu's child. However, the pregnancy was terminated, because our ages combined did not add up to fifty years, and we were not married yet. I was crushed; my heart was broken.

Soon I received a letter from my aunt and my uncle, who were living in America and working at Duke University in North Carolina, where they were both professors. They had gotten me a partial scholarship for Duke, so I went to the American Embassy in Beijing to apply for a visa. I couldn't believe I was actually considering moving to America to live with my aunt and uncle, but my relationship with Lu had been strained since we'd lost our child.

On the application, one of the questions asked whether my parents were members of the Communist Party. My friends had advised me to say no to this question or I wouldn't get a visa. I didn't know what to do. I didn't want to lie, so I left it blank.

"Why did you not answer this question?" the man asked me.

"I don't know."

"Are your parents members of the Communist Party?"

"Yes, they are."

"Are you a member of the Communist Party?"

"No, I'm not."

"Have you applied to be a member?"

"No, I haven't."

"Why not? You're a member of a Red family."

"I don't think I'm qualified," I told him.

I was turned down for the visa. I was told it was because of my age and marital status. I was twenty-one at the time. Not too long after that, I was engaged to be married to Lu.

First he went to his parents; then they spoke with my parents; then he told me. I was the last one on the list to find out that he even wanted to marry me. I was a little upset about being turned down for a visa, but I never even told Lu about my idea of moving to America. I was just happy he wanted to marry me. I knew I wanted a child. I did tell him about the scholarship to Duke University, though. He said I'd still have the opportunity in the future. I wasn't so sure about that. In my experience, if you didn't grab something when it was in front of you, it would be gone.

We had a long engagement, but not as long as it was supposed to be. The first date for our wedding was set for the 1988 Chinese New Year, which would have been in February of 1988. My grandmother flipped out when she heard this. She said this was a blind year. I still don't know exactly what that means, but old Chinese people are very superstitious. So we changed the date to December 23, 1987, so that we would be married before the year ended and before the blind year started.

We were married in a traditional Chinese wedding. My outfit was completely red. My shoes were red, and even the ornaments in my hair were red. The only difference was that my head and face were not covered.

Lu wore a dark blue suit. He was so young and handsome. It was the first time I'd ever seen him in a suit; I'd seen him only in his work uniform or casual clothes. He looked so sophisticated. He came to Zhengzhou in the early morning with three cars to take me, my family, and anyone else I wanted to bring back to Kaifeng, where we were to be married. It couldn't have been better. I had always dreamed of getting married in Kaifeng. We filled the cars with friends and family, and all the relatives were there. It was a huge celebration. It was an amazing day in my life.

IX: A New World

In May of 1989, all our classmates, both mine and Lu's, wanted to go to Beijing to be part of the protest at Tiananmen Square. My father told us it was our job to concentrate on school, not to change the government. We were both still taking college courses.

I'm glad we listened to my father, and I'm sure he was probably scared that we were going to go anyway. He made me stay home for several days in a row while the protest was going on. My father knew what was best for both of us. We finished college. Not long after I found out I was pregnant again, and the pregnancy had to be terminated again. We did not qualify. Now we were married, but we still had the age problem. I was devastated.

At the end of 1989, I was sent by my company to Shijiazhuang, which is right outside Beijing. We had imported machines from America for making tennis shoes. The factory that bought them couldn't get them to operate properly. They needed someone who spoke English to translate. They chose me, because I had been in charge of importing the machines in the first place. During that time, to import or export goods, you had to go through the government. Our company handled all the machinery, equipment, and things like that.

Anyway, the factory with the shoe machines had set them up wrong. They had to fly in technicians from America to recalibrate the machines. Since I knew all about the contract, I was sent to help. This put a strain on my relationship with Lu. We were still like newlyweds; he didn't want me to go anywhere. Nevertheless, I had to go.

Later, that same factory sent me to America. It was the first time I'd ever been outside of China. I'd been all over China, but it was the first time I was to leave the country. I was so excited about going to America and couldn't wait for the day to arrive. No one—not my mother, father, or even my company—thought I'd come back.

"I know you're going to like America," Lu said when I told him about the trip. "You'll probably see your aunt and uncle in North Carolina."

"How am I going to get to North Carolina?" I asked him. "I'm not going to North Carolina."

"Don't you still want to go to Duke University?" he asked.

Then I knew he thought I wasn't coming back, just like everybody else. A distance had grown between us. I had gotten pregnant two other times and had decided to have my tubes tied so I couldn't get pregnant again until the proper time. When our ages allowed us to qualify. We wanted to have a child, and loved each other very much, but it seemed like I was always being sent somewhere far away.

"I love you, Lu. Don't believe what everybody's saying," I told him. "I promise you, I'll be back."

I did go back. One reason is that I felt a responsibility to my country; another reason is that I knew I'd be sent to America again, as well as other places. I was one of the few people at my company who spoke English, and I was also at the top of management.

On this trip, I had to go to world-trade shows in Los Angeles, New York City, Las Vegas, Houston, and several other cities, as well as Hong Kong on my return to China. When I was a child, I'd felt well traveled; now I was world traveled.

I was sent with five other people: four men and one woman. They were all a lot older than I was. I was the only one who spoke English. They were the decision makers, and I was just there to translate. That was fine with me; I was going to America. Ultimately, they really didn't have any power. Anything big that they wanted to do still had to be approved by my company. My company's decision would be made on my recommendation.

I couldn't believe how big our airplane was. I'd never been on an international flight before, and I'd never flown out of the Beijing international airport. I'd been only on small planes on short flights around China. The first thing I noticed was the passengers. They were almost all foreigners. As soon as the flight was in the air, I noticed the second big thing: nobody was speaking Chinese anymore. That's when my job began.

Every time I started to think about anything, say anything, or even do anything, I had to translate for one of my group members. They all had questions at the same time. I had to order all their food, drinks, and anything else they needed; it all went through me. When we were asleep, if one of them had a problem or a question, I would be woken up. By the time we landed in Los Angeles, I was exhausted. They, however, were well rested and full of energy. I tried my best to take in my surroundings, without much luck. Just getting through customs was a nightmare. None of us had ever been through customs. None of us had ever been outside of China.

The oldest man in our group was Mr. Zhao. He was the head of the factory that had purchased the shoe machines. He held everyone's passports.

"Passport, please," the man at customs said.

I looked at Mr. Zhao. He just looked back at me with wonder.

"They need our passports," I told him in Chinese.

He sat his bag on the counter and started to look in it. The man pulled it away from him, dug inside, and pulled out six passports.

"Everyone open your luggage," the man said with a surprised look on his face.

Everyone's luggage was opened and spread out everywhere.

"What's all this about?" Mr. Zhao asked me.

I didn't know what to tell him. I didn't understand what was going on, either. We'd already been through customs when we left China. But it had been nothing like this. They'd just waved us through, and we boarded the plane.

The only things the man found were an apple and two oranges.

"Welcome to America," the man said. He handed us our bags and passports.

"I feel like I was just raped," Mr. Zhao said to me. "I thought Communists were paranoid. Americans are even afraid of fruit."

The next thing one of them noticed was a water fountain.

"What's that?" Mr. Zhao asked me

I didn't know what it was, but when a boy walked up and took a drink, I said, "Oh, that—it's a drinking fountain," like I'd known all along.

"Where are the restrooms?" they asked.

I thought, *Oh, my God!* Once again, my father's training saved me. I proceeded to give a little presentation before anyone went in.

"You didn't tell me about the toilets on the wall," Mr. Zhao said with a huge smile on his face when he came back out.

"What toilets on the wall?" I asked.

"Yes, on the wall," he said. "They have paper in there for you and everything."

"I know, and soap too," I told him. "Did you use the hand dryer?"

Mr. Zhao went straight back into the restroom.

It turns out that the toilets on the wall he was referring to were urinals. Later, he told us he was definitely going to import them into China. "I want to see this toilet paper and these urinals in all the restrooms across China," he told us. "That's what I want to see before I die. Water fountains too."

We all laughed at that.

LAX, the Los Angeles airport, was massive. When we went to get our luggage, we got lost. I asked for directions, but everyone spoke so fast. Plus, I was used to hearing people speak English with a British accent.

When we saw the conveyer belts moving people along, and the carts designed just to hold your luggage, all of us thought America was a rich and smart country. Mr. Zhao wanted to import everything into China, and we hadn't even left the airport yet.

We finally found our consignor. There were so many people, and I was looking everywhere. Everyone in my party kept asking me if we were going the right way. I was so relieved when I finally saw a man holding the sign with the name Zhao on it.

On the way to our hotel, I was taken aback by how tall the buildings were. There were so many tall building, with so much glass. I'd never seen anything like it, with the sun glaring off all that glass. It was amazing to me, to all of us.

We didn't have freeways in China at that time, and we'd never seen so much traffic. Bicycles, yes, but that many cars, no. They all looked new. I couldn't believe how many different kinds of cars there were. In China, all the cars were from China, and they were mostly trucks. When we realized what the carpool lane was, Mr. Zhao said, "They've thought of everything here." He kept pointing out different makes of cars and telling us where they were made.

Oh, and the signs! All the freeway signs telling you exactly where to go. And the billboards advertising everything under the sun. We were like six little kids at an amusement park.

We spent one week in each city. There would always be a day of preparation and then two or three days of trade show. It was very educational. It was also a lot of stress and a lot of work, but I thoroughly enjoyed myself. That trip gave me a completely new perspective on life.

When I was in New York, my aunt and uncle showed up and tried to talk me into leaving with them. They wanted me to stay with them in North Carolina and help them take care of my grandmother. They said I could still attend Duke University on the scholarship they'd obtained for me.

"I'm married now, and I miss my husband. We want to have a child," I told them. "Besides, Mr. Zhao is holding my passport."

"I've already spoken with Mr. Zhao," my aunt said. "He can be a very understanding man."

We'd been told before leaving China that if we had any visitors on this trip, we were to let our leader know. Mr. Zhao was our leader, and I'd already told him my aunt and uncle were there. I didn't know that my aunt had already talked to him, though.

"Just go to his room," my aunt told me. "He's expecting you."

I was a little hesitant about going to his room, but I wanted to see what he had to say.

"Your aunt told me the situation with your grandmother," he began. "I understand you're very close to your grandmother."

"Yes, I am," I told him. "I haven't seen her in four years."

"I'm going to give you your passport and some money," he said. "Whatever you do with it is your choice. I won't look at you differently either way."

"What will you do when you go back to China?" I asked. "What will you tell them?"

"I'm an old man, and I'll be retiring soon," he told me. "I'll just tell them your grandmother is ill, and you have to be with her. I'll be all right."

"Thank you, Mr. Zhao," I said in a voice that let him know I meant it.

"You're young; you have a future. You should go for it," he said. "But I'm not telling you what to do. It's your decision." I knew he was stressing the fact that it was all my decision so that if anything went wrong, he wouldn't have it on his conscience.

We talked for a while. He gave me a lot of good advice. I'd always admired Mr. Zhao. He was a big man with a big heart. When I left his room, I was full of confidence but also confused. I just wasn't sure what I was going to do.

I went to my room and sat on the bed, looking at my passport and the money. He had given me one thousand dollars in American money. That was a fortune to me; I'd never even seen that much money. I had the same feeling I used to have when I picked up discarded vegetables at the vegetable stands when I was a little girl—like I was stealing.

Did I have the right to this passport? I didn't feel right about the money. Then I heard a knock at the door.

"Did you speak with Mr. Zhao?" my aunt asked as I opened the door.

"Yes," I said. I showed her my passport and the money.

"I'm so happy for you. This could change your whole life," she told me with a smile. "I told you Mr. Zhao is an understanding man."

"I don't know if I feel right about any of this," I said as I looked down at the floor.

"You should be happy right now, more than ever," she told me. "You look so sad, Yanyan."

"I'm confused, Aunt. I don't want to get anyone in trouble. I don't feel like this is the right way to do it."

"You're young, and China is changing," she told me. "Everyone is looking for these opportunities. You'll be all right."

"What about my group?" I asked her. "What will they do? None of them speak English."

"Sometimes you just have to worry about yourself," she told me. "They'll find a way."

She told me she had given them her phone number so that they could call her if they had any problems. She told me I should get some rest; we would be leaving early in the morning for North Carolina. She closed the door to my room, and I was alone again. Sitting on my bed, looking at my passport and the money, I didn't know what I was going to do. I didn't sleep the whole night. I kept thinking about so many things. By the time morning came, I knew I would not be leaving with my aunt and uncle.

They couldn't believe I was going back to China. My aunt was stunned. They knew I'd applied for visas in the past. I'd applied for visas to come to America more than once, but I was always turned down.

"You're making the worst mistake of your life, Yanyan," my aunt told me. "Why don't you take a little more time to think about it before you decide?"

"I've made my decision. I don't need more time to think about it," I told her. "I've been thinking about it all night."

"If you go back to China, you'll never see us again," she said. "Think about never seeing your grandmother again."

"I'll be back," I told them, even though I knew they didn't believe me. I wasn't even sure if I believed it. I just knew I couldn't stay there then, not that way.

We cried, and they hugged me. "We'll tell your grandmother you love her and miss her very much," said my aunt before they drove away.

I cried all day. I wasn't sure if my aunt was right. Had I just made the biggest mistake of my life? I felt bad for my grandmother. I'm sure she was expecting them to bring me back.

The next morning, when Mr. Zhao saw that I hadn't left, he got the biggest smile on his face. "I know you've made the right choice," he said as he shook my hand. "You're going to get everything you want, just wait and see."

I didn't know exactly what he meant, then.

When I was in America, I felt everything was different from China. On the plane, flying into Houston, I couldn't believe how much open land I saw from the window. In New York City, so many cars were on the road; it seemed there were as many cars as there were people in China. I was really surprised at the condition of the roads and the organization of the traffic. It wasn't like that in China. Even when I went to Chinatown and ordered kung pao chicken, it was completely different from what I was used to.

I think America is beautiful and very modern, and overall I think the lifestyle is better than it is in China, although homeless people seem to be everywhere in America. In China, you hardly ever see anyone begging for money. I'm not going to say you never see them, but you don't see them nearly as much as I've seen them in America. I know America is a rich country, but they seem to have more homeless and more people in prison than anywhere I have been in the world.

There were no supermarkets in China when I was growing up, only outdoor markets. Farmers would bring their vegetables in carts to sell to the people in the cities. When I went to the supermarket in Los Angles, I couldn't believe it. I'd never seen so much food in one place. All the fruits and vegetables were so clean, shiny, and pretty. I was used to them being dirty, having come right out of the ground; we always had to wash our vegetables before we could eat them. So in Los Angeles, I just had to buy some grapes, apples, and oranges. But when I ate them, they had hardly any taste. I have to say, even though the fruits and vegetables are dirty in China, they taste much better.

When I went to a department store, I saw that everything was made in China, but I had never seen any of these things in my country. There were so many things in one store, in so many different departments. It just wasn't like that in China. We'd been exporting forever, but we hardly imported anything. So I knew right away that I would be going back to China. With my new job, I saw a great opportunity for helping my country.

I started thinking that my people had been getting cheated. I began studying the prices of goods in North America, South America, and Hong Kong. Studying prices was my new thing; this truly was the beginning of free trade. I was shocked at the price markup on the retail end. If China was selling it for twenty cents, it was being resold for twenty dollars. When I went back to China and reported this fact to my company, our prices slowly started to rise.

Free trade has been a great thing for China. I wasn't the only one working on projects like this. My whole country was on fire at the time, alive with all kinds of new business. I loved my first trip to America and was very impressed with the country I'd heard about all my life.

When I returned to China, everyone was surprised, including my husband. They'd been so sure I was going to stay in America. Lu was so happy to see me again. Now that our combined ages reached fifty, we were eligible to have a child.

We had a private, romantic celebration. The next day, I set up an appointment to have my tube-tying operation reversed. I started trying to get pregnant, but nothing happened for a long time. We tried everything. I was so depressed, thinking I would probably never have children.

I was twenty-nine years old, and all of my friends already had children; some of the children were even in elementary school. It had been several years since Lu and I had became eligible to legally have a child, but nothing was happening; there was no bun in the oven.

My mother told me to relax and stop thinking so much about it. My husband told me that if we had a child, it would be great, but if we didn't, that would be all right too. So I just forgot about it and tried to concentrate on him and my work.

I became so obsessed with work that I was moved to the position of top sales manager. But at that time, I wasn't really there for Lu. I was usually away for six months out of the year, which put a lot of strain on our marriage and didn't leave us much time together.

At the end of 1993, I was sent to Beijing for a business trip. Lu had his vacation at the same time, so he went with me. On this trip, I got sick, and all I wanted to do was sleep. He called home to see how the family was doing and told his mother I'd gotten sick and was sleeping all the time.

"Maybe she's pregnant," his mother told him.

And guess what—I was. It had been six years since we'd become eligible to have a child. I had all but given up, and now here I was, pregnant. It was an amazing feeling to know I could have this child with no restraints or restrictions. No one was telling me what I could do with my body. I was twenty-nine years old. I'd thought my chance had passed, and I felt so blessed to be carrying this child. When I started to show, I wore clothes that showed everyone that I was pregnant. I must have been the proudest pregnant woman to ever walk the planet.

Maternity clothes had appeared in China right around that time. Lu was so excited; he told everyone around, "We're pregnant." He wouldn't tell them that *I* was pregnant; he would always say *we*, with the biggest smile on his face. He insisted on taking me to get some maternity clothes, even though I knew I wasn't going to wear them. I was wearing the tightest shirts I could find so that everyone could see my pregnant belly.

X: She Arrives

The families were so happy, completely overjoyed. I was ecstatic, and my husband started taking extra care with me. We didn't want anything to happen to this baby, God forbid. This was our last chance. Lu was always cooking me something good to eat and making sure I was comfortable. Even though I was pregnant, I continued to work. I was always on the phone or going to my office. When I look back, I feel like I probably neglected my husband a lot, but women were not even allowed to work in China until 1949. By the time I was an adult, women were encouraged to work. I was a worker, and I was proud of it.

When I was about six months pregnant, I was sent by my company to trade shows in Guangzhou and Hainan, in the south of China, for one month. While I was there, I got really sick. It shook me up pretty badly; I was afraid I might lose the baby. The doctor tried to give me some pills, but I didn't want to take them, thinking they could hurt the baby.

Then, all at once, I realized nothing in the world mattered anymore except this baby. I'd already told my company this would be my last trip until after I gave birth. When I got back home, I went straight to my doctor to see if everything was all right, and it was. Everything turned out to be fine.

In China, when they do the ultrasound, they are not allowed to tell you the sex, because they're afraid you might do away with it if you know it's a girl. So I didn't know if I was going to have a boy or a girl.

I have heard that there are way more boys than girls in China now because of this kind of thinking. I didn't care if I had a boy or a girl; I just wanted a healthy baby. I slowed down and started letting my husband take

72

care of me the way he wanted to. I was still working but not nearly as much. I would go to work and straight home afterward; he made sure of this.

One day, around my eighth month, I had another big scare. My baby was always moving and kicking. Then one morning, I couldn't feel any movement at all. A few hours went by, and nothing. I got so scared and started to cry. I was home alone, and I couldn't wait for my husband to get home so he could take me to the doctor. When we got there, the doctor examined me and then laughed. "The baby is sleeping," he said. "There's nothing wrong."

"Sleeping all day?" I said.

"Have you never slept all day?" he asked.

Once again, everything was fine.

My due date was supposed to be in the beginning of August, but I didn't deliver until the middle of August. I was huge, my legs and arms were swollen, none of my shoes fit my feet, and my face was fat. Then, on August 10, my water broke in the middle of the night.

My husband took me to the hospital right away, but the doctor said the baby wasn't coming yet. I waited for another whole day and night. It was incredibly uncomfortable. On August 12, the doctor gave me a shot to induce labor and said that if the baby didn't come by the thirteenth, they would have to do surgery. August 12, 1994, was truly the most grueling and painful day and night of my entire life.

I told myself at least a thousand times that day that I'd never have another child as long as I lived. I swear that there were points when I just wanted to die. I had an extremely difficult labor. I saw at least fifteen new mothers come, have their child, and leave, and I was still there.

The doctor made the decision to deliver the baby by C-section and asked my husband to sign the papers saying it was all right. He explained that if he didn't do this, it would be dangerous for me and my baby. They started to prep the operating room and they put an IV in my arm. Suddenly, I started to scream in pain and began to give birth naturally.

I heard the baby cry, and I started crying when they handed her to me. I found myself holding the most beautiful little girl I had ever seen, and she was mine. I forgot about all the pain and suffering I had just gone through. I checked to make sure she had all her tiny little fingers and toes. I couldn't believe how much black hair she had on her head.

I'd seen my friends' and cousins' babies when they were born, and they were very cute, but nothing like this little baby. I felt like she was an angel. I guess every mother feels that way, but my child has been something special.

She was born just before 6:00 p.m. on August 13, 1994, the year of the dog, and given the name Chang Lu, which means happy, joyous, and free. Right away, the family nicknamed her Yangyang, which means morning sunshine.

Once I got her home, she became the center of my everything. Now I know I neglected my husband. All I could see was this beautiful little baby girl. I didn't want to work anymore, I didn't want to answer the phone, and I didn't want to talk to anyone. I didn't want to do anything except watch the baby.

I was absorbed in every little move she made, every little grunt or whimper. Even if she burped, I thought it was brilliant. I was completely obsessed. I think I've probably been obsessed with her since the day she was born. She has become my whole universe.

Under the new Chinese government you were allowed to have only one child, but you were given six months of maternity leave with pay. Under the old rule, when I was born, you could have as many kids as you wanted, but my mother got only fifty-six days of maternity leave. I have thanked the powers that be a million times for this, and I say thank you a million more times. I would never have been able to go back to work that soon. I had the hardest time going back to work. I had the hardest time leaving her at any time at all. I was one of those mothers. I am still one of those mothers. I can't stand it when she's out of my sight. All I do is worry.

It's hard to believe a man can become jealous of a little baby, but it's true. Lu was getting upset, because all I wanted to do was concentrate on the baby. Everything was about her. I have to say, though, he was just as bad.

Every evening for the first six months, friends and family came by to see her. Lu had a couple of lab coats that he made everyone wear if they wanted to hold the baby. He even had gloves for them, and those stretchy things that cover your shoes. It was crazy, but it worked—she never got sick.

When a child reaches one hundred days old in China, there is a huge celebration. Everyone attends, and I mean everyone. People usually bring gifts. Yangyang got so many gifts, and money too. We even opened a bank account for her. It's still there. She doesn't even know about it. That's when I knew she was my good-luck charm. She's always been very special to the family.

When she was born, she was the first girl to arrive. She had a lot of cousins, but they were all boys. Everyone made a big deal about it. My mother and father were so happy to have a granddaughter. There was a time in China when everyone wanted to have boys. I told you, a lot has changed in my life.

I told you before that writing this makes me think of all kinds of stuff. Why is there such a huge celebration for the baby when it reaches one hundred days? I called my father and mother and asked them.

"They call it the one-hundred-day celebration. It's to wish the new child a long and prosperous life," my father told me. "The tradition is so old that I'm not sure why or where it originated."

"Do you think Mom would know?" I asked him. "Can you put her on the phone?"

My mother said basically the same thing. She kept trying to tell me all about my one-hundred-day celebration.

I finally got back on the phone with my father and told him what I thought:

Life was hard in the old days. I suspected that this tradition started in the 1700s or early 1800s, maybe even before that. If your child lived one hundred days, then the chances were good that it would survive. But I bet a lot of babies died back then, from hunger, sickness, cold, bad weather, and even birth itself.

My grandmother told me she lost two babies at birth, before my father was born. There were no hospitals, and I'm sure there weren't many doctors. Plus, you had to pay them. And what kind of equipment would they have? Can you imagine? All we can do is imagine.

My grandmother told me about giving birth to my father during World War II. She said the Japanese were bombing China every day. She said when the sirens went off, they would all run for the bomb shelters. She was seven months pregnant, running down the street with her husband and two boys—one was eight and one was four—when her water broke.

She said they ran into a temple, and she gave birth to my father right there with his father and two brothers watching. She said my grandfather cut the cord and tied it in a knot, and they took their new baby and went to the bomb shelter.

That's what my grandmother said. This is what I'm saying. All we can do is imagine. My father is lucky that he even survived at all. He just turned seventy years old. Happy birthday, Dad.

Before Yangyang was born, I was obsessed with work. Maybe I wasn't obsessed, but I was definitely overachieving. There was no incentive at my job at that time. It wasn't like I was going to get more pay, more vacation time, or anything like that. I did have the privilege of traveling, but that was it.

Now I didn't want to work at all. I couldn't stand being away from my daughter. Six months went by too fast. I never used to go home during the day when I was at work. Luckily I lived nearby and was in management, because now I found myself going home once or even twice during the day. Sometimes I said I had a meeting with a client when it wasn't even true. I was breastfeeding, so I was allowed one trip home at lunchtime. But this wasn't enough.

Several weeks after I returned to work, I was told that my company was setting up a branch in Houston, Texas, in the United States of America! I thought this was my chance, the chance of a lifetime. A chance that everyone dreams about. A chance to go to America and live there legally.

I had been to America. I knew what this could mean for my daughter. I knew what this could mean for me and my family. The problem was that the thought of leaving her even for one day was too much to bear. Also, I was still breastfeeding. I told my company that my baby was too little to leave right now. I asked them if they could wait until she was one year old. They told me they would discuss it and let me know but warned me that I could lose this opportunity. At that time in China, when you worked for the government and they asked you to do something, it was really them telling you to do it.

I went home crying. I've never had a feeling like that before or since. To have one of the greatest dreams of my life coming true, but to have to give up something so precious to me to get it—I didn't know what to do. Lu told me I should go; he knew this had always been my dream. Plus, this was truly the chance of a lifetime. I told him what I had told my company. He thought I was crazy and said they'd never go for that. He said they'd probably want me to leave right away. That was an emotional evening for both of us. A lot of tears fell that night between me and Lu.

A few weeks later, I was called into the main office one morning for a meeting. They told me I could wait until my baby was one year old. I was so happy and so sad. Now I knew I was really going to leave her. I didn't even know how long it would be before I could get her to America. I had already been looking at her and crying all the time. How could I start thinking about a new life in a new country when she would still be in China?

Slowly I started to arrange things for the big day of my departure. I tried to teach her how to walk, talk, and everything. I wanted to be the one who taught her all these things.

It's so hard to write about this. I wanted a child so badly; I waited for so long. Now I had her, and I was going to leave my beautiful angel. But it would have been impossible for me to say no. There are no words to explain my feelings. It just once again makes me think of how my parents were separated for all those years. It makes me understand so many things.

I was counting down every day. My daughter went from representing joy to representing sadness. Every time I held her, I cried. When she was eleven months old, she started saying "mama" and "baba." I was so pleased with myself and with her. By twelve months, she was walking.

I thought I was about to leave her, but the week before I was supposed to leave, my visa had not been cleared. This was excellent, because I was going to have to leave right after her birthday. Now I didn't know when I was going to leave; all I knew was that every day was an extra day with her.

At thirteen months, she was running around the house and saying several words. At fourteen months, she was even singing. Then I was told I had to leave. How was I going to do this? What in the world was going on? I couldn't have been more dazed and confused. I was an absolute emotional wreck.

Thinking back on it now, I'm not sure how I managed. I get anxiety attacks just thinking about it. I do remember it came down to hours, and then minutes. The last thing I saw at the airport was her father holding her. The last thing I heard her say was, "Mama, zaijia," which means good-bye in Chinese. Then she was gone. And my heart burst.

To this day, I don't remember that flight to America. I don't remember getting on the plane in China; I don't remember arriving in Houston. Everything is just blank. I barely remember my first few days in Houston. I remember that everyone thought I had hay fever, because my eyes were so puffy and red from crying.

I was six months old in this photo.

My mom and dad's wedding photo

My mom (right) with her family

My dad (back left) with his family, with my mom standing to his left.
This was before they were married.

My parents during the Chinese Cultural Revolution

The grapevine in Kaifeng

My father (right) with his siblings

Always with Mom

My mom (center) doing theater

This temple is from the Dong Zhou Dynasty 东周 (東周 770-221 **B.C.**)

A baby in Beijing

My father and I in Beijing

My father with his gymnastics team

TV show, 1981. My father was a judge.

My father with Jet Li's coach. This is the only photo I
could find of an Olympic training facility.

I tried to get into the army and got the uniform and everything.
They rejected me because I was an only child.

My mom and me visiting my dad in Zhengzhou

One of the many ways to get around in China

Playing in the park with my dad

My parents. Mom was five months pregnant with me.

Lu and me, the summer we started dating

Mr. Zhao

My one-hundred-day celebration

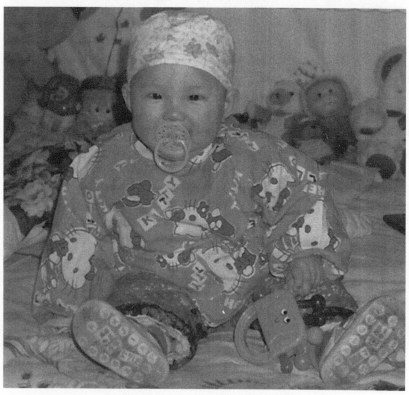

Yvonne's one-hundred-day celebration

Pictures that were sent to me when I first arrived in America

Having a blast

My little girl is coming to America

The day I married Tony

Twinkle, twinkle, little star

The little handful

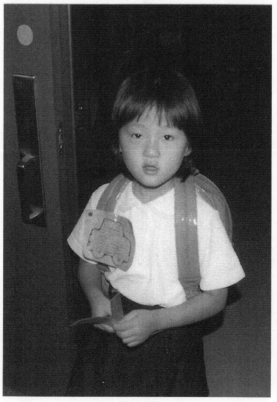

First day of preschool

Kitty cat

Makeup for Disney

Cold Case

Skating at Pickwick

Homework between filming

Film shoot for 2008 Olympics commercial

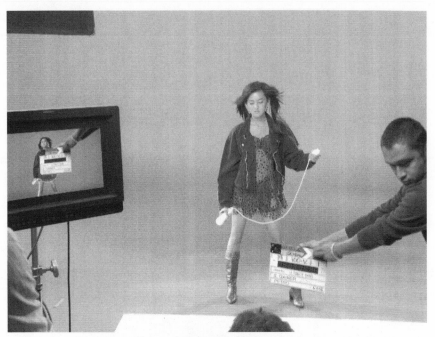

Wii video game

LA Marathon

"Go green" commercial shoot

Hannah Montana

Revamped

Troubled teen

Three generations in San Francisco

Award ceremony at the Chinese Embassy in Houston, Texas

Journey to the West film shoot

She made it to the Olympic stadium a little too late.

Those used to be my sunglasses.

Verizon commercial filming in Malibu

Award ceremony for *Still the Drums*

XI: She Was Gone

I really threw myself into my work this time. I spoke English, but it was British English; in America, they speak differently. I had to learn to drive. I had to learn about my new surroundings. I started to feel okay except when I was alone. After work sometimes, I would just go home and sit and cry. I knew I wasn't doing her any good this way; I had to get my act together. Otherwise, I was never going to get her to America with me.

Sometimes in the evenings, I would sit at home and squeeze the milk from my breasts and just cry. I knew she was in China, and she needed her mother.

When I saw another woman with her baby, I would die a little bit inside. The whole situation was a nightmare that I just wanted to wake up from. When I called home to see how she was doing, my husband told me that every time she saw a plane in the sky, she'd point and say, "Mama." This totally killed me. I almost became useless.

I was reprimanded at my job for being unfocused. I had also left work early for several days; I was so depressed that I just couldn't handle it. But when they reprimanded me, I got scared. I realized that if I didn't get it together soon, I was going to blow everything I had worked for.

I felt so tired. I was always waking up in the middle of the night, hearing her saying, "Bye bye, Mama," in that same little voice I'd heard at the airport the day I left her.

I wrote a letter home to my mother and told her how hard a time I was having. She had a good idea. She told me she'd get a tape recorder and record Yangyang playing and singing. I couldn't wait to get the tape, but when I did, and I listened to it, it made things worse.

I called my company back in China and told them I couldn't take it. I needed to see my family soon. They said I would be receiving a letter, explaining how things were changing in China. I did receive that letter. It had been only eight months since I'd left China. My mother and my husband had told me things were changing fast. I had no idea. The letter said that my company would be privatizing soon. This was happening all over China. It was a disaster for me.

When my company was owned by the government, all my expenses were paid for. My car, my rent, everything, plus five hundred dollars a month. I was also still getting paid my monthly salary back in China. Now, however, I wasn't even sure how much I'd be making each month. I knew from now on I'd have to pay all my own expenses. I was on my own.

My husband was working for the government, too, in a more sensitive area than I was. His getting a visa to come to America would not be easy. First, he would have to obtain passports for himself and Yangyang. He managed to do this, but visas were another problem. He gave up his government position. This was almost unheard of in China, but he did it, just to get the passports. With my husband no longer working for the government, I could have just asked my company to grant my husband and my child a visit to America, but it was no longer possible.

When my company became privately owned and was no longer part of the government, the only way for me to keep my job was to go back to China. There was no way I was going back to China. I had come too far and sacrificed too much. I wanted to raise my daughter in America. But how was I going to get her here?

I called my husband back in China. He said he was having no luck at all obtaining visas. I had taken a job doing antique appraisals, dealing with Asian antiques. Since I didn't have citizenship, the job paid cash, and it wasn't much, since it was under the table. The time on my own visa was running out, my passport was still being held by the Chinese government, and I missed my little girl more than ever. I didn't know what I was going to do.

I talked to an attorney who told me I could make a plea to the American government saying that I wanted more children, which would not be allowed if I lived in China. But I didn't want to go against my country in any way. I told him that my biggest dream in life was to raise my child in America.

"The only other way would be if you can find an import/export company in America that will hire you for your knowledge of the Chinese market," he told me. "At least then you'll be able to extend your visa and give you more time to figure out how we're going to get your family here."

I set out right away trying to find that job. That's like looking for a needle in a haystack. I talked to anyone and everyone who would listen to my dilemma.

My aunt and uncle, along with my grandmother, had moved from North Carolina to Dallas by that time. My aunt offered to buy me a plane ticket to visit them. She said she and my uncle would help me figure something out. I decided to go for the weekend. My roommate dropped me off at the airport. I was a little apprehensive about the whole thing. I had twenty-five dollars in my pocket, time was running out, my money was running out, and I wasn't sure this was the answer. Ultimately, I didn't get any answers in Dallas, but I'm glad I went. It was great to see my grandmother and my aunt's family.

When I returned to Houston, my roommate didn't come to pick me up. When I called her to ask where she was, she told me she wasn't going to make it. She'd been in an accident, and they had towed her car.

I didn't know what I was going to do. I was down to eight dollars, so there was no way I could get a cab. I thought of a client from the antiques shop who was always flirting with me and telling me if I ever needed anything, anything at all, at any time, to call him. His name is Tony. I decided to put him to the test. I called, and he came right away. He showed up in a huge car. I didn't know at the time that it was a limousine. It was the first time I'd ever seen a limo. It turns out he was the owner of a limo company. I thought he must be rich. I'd never been in such a luxurious car. Tony is an average guy; he never overdresses or wears jewels or anything fancy. He always has a cap on his head. He's not the kind of guy who stands out in a crowd. He took me to dinner, even though I wasn't really in the mood. He insisted, so I decided I'd bore him with all my problems.

He told me he had an attorney friend who dealt with setting up corporations. He said he was interested in starting a business, and that if he did, he could hire me to manage it. I thought it was all too good to be true. I tried not to get my hopes up. I figured he was only interested in one thing, if you know what I mean. We finished dinner, and I thanked him for a nice evening and for the ride. When he dropped me off at my house, he asked for my phone number.

"I don't think that's a good idea," I told him.

"No, I mean for business," he said. "I'm serious about starting this new company."

I gave him my pager number instead of my phone number. I only ever saw three different phone numbers on my pager.

A few weeks later, my pager went off, showing a number I'd never seen before. I called, and it was a job offer from Tony. He'd started that new company and wanted me to manage it. He suggested I talk to a lawyer right away about fixing my visa.

I spoke with my attorney. By this time I had my own, believe me. I can't even tell you all the phone calls and meetings and hoops I had to jump through. But I was overjoyed to find out that my attorney would start the process that would eventually lead to my being an American citizen.

My next move was to start the process of getting visas for my daughter and husband. The attorney told me I'd have to write a formal letter to the American Embassy in China, requesting visas for my two immediate family members. He said I'd also have to have a certain amount of money in the bank to show that I would be able to support them for the three months they'd be here. On top of that, I'd need the owner of the company, Tony, to sign the right papers that would allow this to happen.

I didn't know how I was going to approach Tony about this. I knew he liked me as more than just an employee or a friend. I did nothing to encourage this. He would ask me to go different places with him after work, but I would always find a reason to say no.

Tony is Iranian; he came to America in 1974. In March, Iranians celebrate the new year. He invited me to a big celebration in the park with all his Iranian friends. This time, I decided to say yes. I needed to get out and do something to get my mind off all the stress I'd been facing the fact that I missed Yangyang so much.

When we were there, I saw all the families with children—mothers with little babies, all the husbands and grandparents, everyone together. I started crying and couldn't stop; I couldn't control myself. Tony saw me crying and asked what was wrong. I told him I missed my family so much that it was starting to drive me crazy.

"That's it," he said. "We've got to figure out how to get them here."

"I've found a way," I told him, "but I'm not sure you'll want to do it."

He told me to explain, so I told him the whole situation. I told him I'd need him to sign those papers or I would have to have his life. I didn't really say this, but in the condition I was in, I might have. But the truth is, Tony was always so good to me. He had no problem signing the papers.

I called Lu and told him to get ready to see America. When he asked how, I explained the whole situation. I told him he'd receive documents in the mail soon and that he and Yangyang would have to go to the American Embassy in Beijing to obtain their visas. I could tell he was happy but that he was also suspicious of Tony.

Not long after this, he called from Beijing. "I have them in my hand right now, two visas," Lu said. "One for me and one for Yangyang." I'll never forget the happiness in his voice. He told me he'd be coming with Yangyang in two months. I fell to my knees and touched the ground. My baby girl was going to be on American soil.

XII: Girlfriends, and the Way Life Is

Then Lu told me he had a friend who had moved to Los Angeles and that she wanted to talk to me about living in America. He asked if it would be all right if she called, and I said yes. When she called, though, she didn't ask me about living in America. Instead, she proceeded to tell me that she was my husband's girlfriend.

I was a little surprised, but not really. Lu must have been as lost and lonely as I had been. But that still didn't make things any easier. I'd heard rumors from my friends in China about him being with another woman, but I hadn't wanted to believe it. I was so happy that I was going to see my little girl, but I was so sad that I might lose my husband.

I have always had these extremes in my life. Why can't I just be happy or sad? These feelings seem to always be together. I'm happy about one thing and sad about something else. Anyway, I got on the phone and called Lu.

"So you have a new girlfriend," I said when I heard him on the other end of the line.

"Of course not," he said. "What are you talking about?"

"Your friend called me," I told him. "She told me everything."

He tried to deny it again. Then he finally told me the truth. He said that since I'd left China, things had been very different for him. Everyone thought I was never coming back, so they thought he would be leaving soon. Even at his job, he had become less important. He said he missed me so much and was so lonely when he met her.

"There's no way I can forgive you," I told him. "Look what you've done to our family."

"We can talk about it when I get to America," he said.

I started to cry. I thought my marriage was over, but I couldn't wait to see Yangyang.

In the meantime, I was doing really well at my new job with Tony and was also still working as an antiques appraiser. Plus, I was a receptionist at a doctor's office on the weekend. I wanted to put up as much money as I could for me and my little girl.

I kept thinking that I was going to be a single mother. Even though she was coming for only a six-month period, I knew my child was never going back to China. I'd talked to my attorney, and he said it might be possible for me to get her visa extended for six more months. I didn't care what I had to do. I wasn't going to give her up again. I was tired and depressed but full of hope.

One morning, I couldn't get out of bed. I was supposed to go with Tony to meet a client, but I'd been up all night crying. The truth about Lu was finally hitting me. He was the father of my child—the man I loved so much; he was my first love. I'd thought we'd be together forever. He was supposed to always be there for me.

When Tony called, I told him I was sick. He came right over and asked if I needed to see a doctor. He'd never been inside my house. I went out to meet him. I must have looked a mess. I couldn't hide it anymore. I broke down and told him everything.

"Don't worry about anything," he said. "I'm going to take care of you and your child."

I felt like a bird with a broken wing that had been caught in this man's trap. I think it was the weakest point of my life. I know he helped me in so many ways, more than I could ever say. If it hadn't been for Tony, I would never have gotten my baby here. But I found myself in a position of being more and more dependent on him. He has a son from a previous marriage. His name is Amir. It made me wonder what happened to that marriage. But who am I to be suspicious? My marriage with Lu seemed to be falling apart.

I didn't want to be living with a roommate when Lu and Yangyang came, so I started looking for a house to buy. I could afford only a one-bedroom. This would have been fine, but Tony said I probably should get a two-bedroom. He knew I was bound and determined to keep my family here. He said he'd help me and that I could pay him back through the company.

Tony got a realtor for me to start showing me two-bedroom houses. It had been a year and four months since I'd arrived in America. I'd been working seven days a week the entire time and had saved up every bit of money I could. Here I was in Houston, Texas, in the United States of America, and I was about to buy my first house.

Those first days after I'd arrived in Houston had been so dark for me; I'd been certain my life was over. Now Yangyang and Lu were coming, and I was buying a new townhouse for us to live in. That's right—I'd found a perfect little townhouse. I was so proud of myself. All those days when I'd been working so hard, I'd had no idea if anything was going to go my way. Now everything seemed to be falling into place. Except the situation with my husband. That was something I was still going to have to deal with.

Escrow closed on the house twenty days before Lu and Yangyang arrived. I spent all my free time making everything just right. If I wasn't working at my job, I was working on my new house. I was so tired, but I couldn't have been happier. All I knew was that she was coming. Nothing else mattered.

I had no furniture and no money left to buy furniture. Then one day, Tony showed up and said he had a house-warming gift for me. It was a truck full of furniture. He said there was no way he was going to let me live in an empty house. There was a couch, chairs, and a coffee table for the living room; a kitchen table with chairs; and a bed.

Two of my girlfriends had already brought me a bunch of dishes, including pots and pans. Now everything was really complete. It was the first time since I'd been in America that I felt like I was home. All I needed now was her.

I was counting every day, every minute. It was like waiting for something that was never going to come. I couldn't sleep, even though I was dead on my feet. I acted as though staring at the calendar would make the days go by faster. There is no way I can describe how I really felt.

Four days before they were to arrive, I got a knock on my door at 3:00 a.m.

"Are you Yanyan Yang?" a policeman asked.

"I am," I said. "Can I help you?"

"Can you step outside, please?" he asked.

There were police cars everywhere, along with two ambulances. Then I saw it. My car had been hit. Three young boys were being loaded into the ambulances. They had hit my car and then hit a power pole.

I felt bad for the boys; they'd been driving drunk. I felt worse for myself when I realized I wouldn't be able to drive my car anymore. All I could think about was how I was going to get to the airport.

I had no way to get to work the next morning, so I called Tony and told him what had happened. He told me he had a friend who owned an impound yard, where I could store the car until I figured out what to do. When the car was towed, I found out there was no way to fix it. It was a total loss.

I called the insurance company and eventually came out ahead. What an ordeal, though! I asked them about a rental car, but they told me no, because the owner of the other car didn't have full coverage. I didn't have full coverage, either, but I called my insurance company anyway. I told them what had happened and that my family would be arriving from China in three days. I told them I needed a car. They told me it would be impossible but that they'd send an adjuster the next day.

The next day, I met the adjuster at the impound yard, and he wrote me a check for eighteen hundred dollars. Now I had two days to find a car. Tony suggested I go to a car auction, since I had so little money. An auction was being held the very next day. I asked Tony to take me. I bought a light-blue 1992 Ford Escort. It was running, but it had some problems, so I couldn't drive it right away.

I know all of this sounds average and trivial now. But for me at that time, it was a lot of firsts. My first car, my first accident (luckily I hadn't been in the car). My first time dealing with an insurance company and an adjuster. The first time the police ever knocked on my door. I remember that when they asked me if I was Yanyan Yang, I found it strange—I hadn't heard that name since I was in China. Everyone calls me Grace here in America. When I first started working at the antique company, the owner Mr. Wishnow didn't want to call me Yanyan, he said, "You look like a Grace to me," and the name just stuck.

I still had the same dilemma, though. My husband and daughter were arriving the next day, and I had no car to drive. I called my girlfriends. I had only two at the time, and both of them were busy with work. My only other option was Tony. I knew it was going to be awkward. There was so much going on between me and Lu, and I hadn't seen him and Yangyang in so long.

I had gotten two more phone calls from Lu's new girlfriend. She was still living in Los Angeles and wanted to let me know that they were in love with each other. I knew Lu had a layover in Los Angeles, and it drove me crazy to think that she was going to see Yangyang before I was. My mother had told me that Lu had a suitcase full of things from her mother, and he was supposed to meet her at the airport in Los Angeles so she could get them from him.

I knew at this point that my marriage was over. I wanted so badly to just pick them up by myself. It's funny: in life, no matter how well everything is going for you, something always seems to be out of place. I had to make a phone call and tell Tony that my husband had a girlfriend. I couldn't tell him face to face. It was one of the hardest phone calls I've ever made.

Then the time finally came! I remember it so clearly. Tony did drive me to the airport. When I saw Yangyang and her father, she was crying in his arms. I think she was tired and uncomfortable from the long flight. Lu handed her to me. When I held her, I couldn't talk. My tears were like a waterfall. I tried to talk, but I couldn't say a word. She looked at me and started to cry more. I was crying, she was crying.

We held each other that way for a long time. Then I looked at my husband; he was crying too. He came over and hugged both of us. Then my tears became a river. I completely broke down. Now there were sounds coming out of my mouth that weren't words. All those years, all those emotions, everything at once—it all hit me. It was incredibly relieving, like a weight off my shoulders. I'd been carrying around the fact that I didn't have my child like a piece of heavy luggage. We stood there that way for I don't know how long, until I finally remembered Tony was there. Then I noticed that he was crying, too.

"I'm sorry," I said, looking his way. "I guess we need to go now."

"It's all right," he said, wiping the tears from his eyes. "Take all the time you need. I'm in no hurry."

That night, the three of us lay in bed together: me on one side, my husband on the other, and Yangyang in the middle. They were both sound asleep from the jetlag. I couldn't sleep at all. I just looked at her and touched every little part of her little body.

In the one and a half years since I'd seen her, I could tell she'd grown so much. When I held her, she felt so much bigger. Her head was on my arm, and I kept kissing her face, her eyes, her nose, her little ears, everywhere. I was crying and talking to her.

Then I realized that this baby was beautiful. I was looking at the prettiest little Chinese girl I had ever seen. I had my baby back; I was completely overwhelmed. I looked at my husband. He was sound asleep and snoring. His face was as handsome as it had ever been, but I felt so distant from him. Things were not supposed to be this way.

The next morning, Tony brought my new car. It was all clean and ready to go. Everything was so awkward, though. My husband had a girlfriend, and I had this guy helping me with everything.

My main concern was Yangyang. I felt like my husband had drawn the battle line and had drawn first blood. I was not really that concerned with his feelings anymore. I called my parents and told them everything. I told them about his girlfriend and that I thought I wanted a divorce. It all seemed like a setup to me, how she had moved here just five months earlier. Maybe that was why Lu had had such a hard time getting visas for him and Yangyang. Maybe he'd just been spending time with that woman.

My father said I should give it some time. He told me that Lu and I had been apart from each other for so long and that Lu was young and inexperienced. "Life is long, and you're starting a new life in a new country," he told me. "You have a child together. You're supposed to be united." My father almost had me convinced; he always makes so much sense.

Then she called again. My husband had the nerve to ask if she could visit so we could all talk.

I almost hit the roof, but then I thought, *Why not?* I wanted to see how they acted toward each other. I wanted to see if what she'd said was true. Were they really in love? So I said yes.

Looking back, I think I may have made the wrong decision. When I told Tony she was coming, I could see he was happy. But I wasn't.

In the meantime, I showed Lu and Yangyang around Houston. I showed them the Houston Museum and where I used to live and work. Yangyang was a blast to be around. She was two and a half years old now, full of energy. Then I started talking with Lu about China and how I'd missed my parents, him, and Yangyang. I asked how his parents were doing. The conversation did not stay light for long. Soon we were arguing. I'd known it was coming, I just hadn't known when.

"Why do you feel like you need this other woman in your life?" I asked him.

"I know you're seeing Tony," he said.

"Are you crazy? Tony is a great person," I told him. "He helped me so much when no one else was there. He's just a good friend, and only a friend."

"He sure has done a lot for you," Lu said, "for him to be just a friend."

"Yes, a friend to me, you, and Yangyang," I told him. "You wouldn't be in America right now if it wasn't for what Tony has done."

"I didn't want to come to America," he told me. "You should have come back to China, to your husband and child."

"I'm never moving back to China, and neither is Yangyang," I told him. "To visit my parents, yes, but to live there, no!" I could see by the look on his face that we were going to have problems.

His girlfriend arrived the next day. Lu went with Tony to the airport to pick her up. I know this was awkward for Tony. Lu didn't speak much English at the time, and I don't think his girlfriend did, either.

"Just pretend you're a limo driver, Tony," I said. "I refuse to go."

"You're going to have to meet her anyway," Tony told me. "You might as well meet her now."

"I'd rather meet her at my own house," I said, "on my own terms."

They took Yangyang with them to the airport, and I went to work. I decided this woman was not going to disturb my life anymore than she already was.

When I left work, it was hard to go home, knowing she would be there. When I walked in the door, she and Lu were in the kitchen with Yangyang. Lu had made dinner, and they were waiting for me.

The first thing I noticed was Yangyang sitting on her lap. She seemed so familiar with her. I grabbed Yangyang. "Hi, baby," I said as I picked her up.

"See my aunt," Yangyang said, pointing over her shoulder.

I was so mad and jealous. My child knew her better than she knew me. But I knew all of that was going to change soon!

That night, I made the girlfriend a bed on the couch downstairs in the living room. I slept with Yangyang in my room, and my husband slept in Yangyang's room. When I woke up the next morning, the girlfriend wasn't downstairs. She was in Yangyang's room with Lu.

I left to go to work, but instead I called my girlfriend and told her what I'd been going through. Sometimes you get a lot of strength from friends. She turned out to be a good friend with a lot of good advice. After talking with her, I went to find a daycare center for Yangyang. I knew that Lu was going to have to leave my house with that woman.

When I went home that evening, Lu told me he wanted to take Yangyang back to Los Angeles to see friends we had who were living there. I told him that if he could wait two weeks, I'd be able to go with them. For some reason, he had to go right then.

"Leave, then," I told him. "But you're not taking Yangyang anywhere."

That night, I taught Yangyang her first three English words: *pee pee*, *thirsty*, and *hungry*. As long as she could say these three things, I thought she would be all right.

The next morning, I dropped her off at daycare. Then I went and bought two plane tickets to Los Angeles. I drove straight to my house and handed Lu the tickets. I called Tony and told him he was going to have to drive Lu and his girlfriend to the airport. "I'm not driving them anywhere," I told him, "and my marriage is over."

Tony picked them up. I was so glad that Yangyang was at her new daycare, because as soon as the door closed behind them, I lost control of my emotions. I'd been so strong and straight-faced since seeing that woman in my kitchen, but now I was a complete wreck.

My man was gone, and I was alone. Sure, I had my little girl, and she meant everything to me. But now I was going to be raising her alone. How was I going to tell her where her daddy went? I lay on my living room floor for a long time, crying and feeling sorry for myself. Then I started thinking, *Wait a minute. I don't need him—I need her, Yangyang, and I've got her.* I pulled myself up off the floor and tried to get my act together.

It worked for a little while. I picked Yangyang up from daycare and we had a bite to eat. At home, I started to clean and put some things away while she was playing, doing anything to keep my mind occupied. That night, when I put her to bed, something happened. I think I had a mild breakdown. I don't even know if you would call it mild. This is when I truly started having feelings for Tony.

I completely crashed. It was unreal. Everything had happened so fast. Lu was here, and now he was gone. My stress level was at an all-time high. I couldn't get out of bed, and I was on an emotional roller coaster ride. I was supposed to work with Tony that day, but I didn't show up. The only time Yangyang and I got out of bed was to use the bathroom or get something to eat. She did this twice. I didn't eat anything that day; I had no appetite. It took everything I had just to make it to the kitchen with her.

When Tony called to see where I was, I told him I was sick. He said he'd see me the next morning.

The next morning, he didn't hear from me, and neither did my other job at the antiques company. By that evening, Tony was at my door with flowers and some groceries. He asked me if I was hungry. I hadn't eaten in two days, but I wasn't hungry. I was just numb.

He came in and started cooking something for Yangyang. "Are you all right?" he asked. "You look a little pale."

"I'm not sure," I told him. "I have no energy at all, and I feel dizzy."

"You probably need to eat," he told me.

"I know I need to eat," I said, "but I have no appetite."

He told me to sit down at the table, and he would have dinner ready right away. He stayed for a little while after dinner. Not long, though. I told him I wanted to be alone.

The next day, I called my boss at the antiques company and told him everything that had happened. I asked him if it would be okay if I took a few personal days. He asked me how long I'd be gone. I told him to call if he really needed me.

I think I just wanted to be alone with my daughter. I know I wasn't functioning very well at all. I called the dentist's office where I had been working part-time and told them I would have to quit. I told them that I had my daughter here in America now. I wouldn't have time to work there anymore.

I moped around the house and played with her for three days, kind of in a fog. Tony came by to cook dinner and make sure Yangyang got breakfast each morning. He didn't live that close, but I knew how he felt about me by then. He didn't mind, and he seemed to love being around Yangyang. I could tell he was a family man; he knew just how to deal with her. He was really good in the kitchen too. The food he made was great, and he never left a mess. He would wash the dishes and everything. Things were a lot easier with him around.

On the evening of the third day, I got a call. It was my boss from the antiques company, saying there was an important client coming who spoke only Chinese. He needed me to come in the next morning to translate. I told him I'd be there.

It took everything I had the next morning to get myself up and go to work. I couldn't believe it. I've never been so weak and useless in my whole life. I had Yangyang in the car with me, and I almost forgot to drop her off at daycare. I made it through that meeting and told my boss I was going back home. I told him to call me if he needed me. I said I'd let him know when I was feeling better.

I remember driving home, feeling like a zombie. I continued this way for over a month. All I could do was think about my husband with that woman and my child without her father. My life had turned upside down.

I couldn't focus on anything. Every time I looked at her, I just felt so bad for her and for me.

In the meantime, I wasn't making any money, and I still had bills to pay. Even though my house was paid for, I was still supposed to pay Tony back the money he'd helped me with. He'd said I could work it off through his company, but now I'd almost abandoned his company. I knew at this point he was trying to get close to me. He wasn't hiding it anymore. I still had my power bill, my phone bill, Yangyang's daycare, and food to buy. Tony was paying for all of this. What a great guy; I couldn't believe I'd been blessed with such a good friend. I knew he wanted more, but I gave him no indication that there would ever be anything more.

Still, he continued to help in any way he could. Yangyang started to speak English pretty well. She was at daycare every day, around nothing but English. Tony spoke only English to her. I guess I was the only one at that time who spoke to her in Chinese. Every day she would sing "Twinkle, Twinkle, Little Star." She ended up in the choir at her daycare.

I was so proud: she had taught her teacher and the other children how to speak some Chinese. She seemed to adjust so well. She did have one little problem, though. Her teacher said she had to hide all the scissors from Yangyang or she'd start cutting her own hair. I had to laugh when I heard this. I'd just found her two nights before in the bathroom at home, cutting her bangs to the point where she had none left. When I took the scissors from her, I asked, "Yangyang, what are you doing?"

"Look," she said. "I'm pretty, Mommy."

It was hilarious, and I needed a good laugh.

I'd almost missed Yangyang's first birthday, and I did miss her second birthday. Now it was August, and it would soon be her third birthday. Her first birthday in America. I felt so bad, though. On her first and second birthdays, she'd had so many people there: her grandparents, her father, her cousins, aunts, uncles, and friends. Even I'd been there for her first birthday. On her third birthday, I was going to be the only family member there. This was no good. All I'd been doing was crying about losing her father.

I wouldn't say I was a great mother those first few months. When I was alone in America, all I could think about was her and how I was going to get her and Lu here. Now we were all in America, and our daughter was about to have her third birthday. But we were separated: Yangyang and I were in Houston, and he was in Los Angeles with that woman. What a total disaster my life had become.

Tony had a great idea, though. We decided to invite children from her daycare, my friends' children, and some of his friends' children. It was perfect, and everyone had a great time. She didn't care who anybody was. She was just glad that all those people had come to see her.

Our house had been so gloomy since her father had left, but now it was full of excitement. I felt so good for her that day; there was a new light in her eyes. Happy birthday, Yangyang. I'm glad she had a great day that day, because I didn't. Even though my house was full of people, even though it was my child's third birthday, I could not have felt lonelier. I missed her father, and I missed my parents.

After everyone left, my house was quiet again. Yangyang was exhausted from the day's activities. I watched her lying on the bed, holding a new baby doll. She had a smile on her face, even though she was fast asleep. I thought of Niuniu, the baby doll I'd had when I was little like her. Then I broke down sobbing again.

Did I make a mistake? Had I acted too quickly, all because of pride and ego? Should I have fought harder for my husband? Would it have changed anything? Would he have still left with that woman? I had traveled so far since I was that little girl with my baby doll back in China. But I was still so confused about life. I am still confused about life.

That night, I decided to call my parents. After talking with them, I even called Lu's mother. I think I still had hope that I could save my marriage. When I'd talked to his mother in the past, she'd always been supportive, telling me that her son was stupid and immature and that he should be concerned only with his wife and his child. This time, she changed her tone.

"We are old, you are growing," she told me. "We are in China, you are in America. There is nothing I can do."

When I hung up, I had no more hope. I could tell by the way she had spoken to me that Lu had told her his feelings. I called my parents back right away. I told them I had spoken with Lu's mother and that I was going to file for divorce.

"You should have been calling your husband instead of his mother," my father told me. "If both of you weren't married to your pride, you'd still be married to each other. You're both acting like idiots."

"He's the idiot," I said. "Lu is totally in the wrong."

"Call your husband before you make any more stupid mistakes," my father said.

"Why should I call him? He's the one with a girlfriend. He's in the wrong. He should be calling me and saying sorry."

"You need to pull yourself together. You need to be strong for Yangyang," my father said. "You're in another country now. I'm not there to help you."

"Don't worry about Yangyang and me," I told him. "Things are a lot easier in America than they are in China. I just don't want to raise my daughter without a father."

Then I told him about Tony and how he'd been helping me in so many ways. My father got mad and gave the phone to my mother. My mother told me to send a picture of Tony immediately so that she could take it to the fortune teller.

In China, we believe this stuff; in America, only the superstitious people believe. But there are a lot of superstitious people, and I am one of them. I didn't even realize it until I was writing this book.

When I was fourteen years old, two girlfriends and I went to a fortune teller in Kaifeng. She told me I had a lot of children in me, but only one of them was alive, and it would be born if my parents, grandparents, and I had good hearts. She also said I was going to live my life far away from the city I was born in. I asked her how far—like Beijing? She said no, on the other side of the world. I remember my friends and I laughing at that old blind lady. We thought she was crazy; at that time, nobody in China was leaving to go anywhere else to live. Then the fortune teller got quiet and held my right hand tightly. She started rubbing the palm of my hand, up and down each finger.

"What is the year, month, and day of your birth?" she asked. This was strange; I'd given her my birth date and birth name in the beginning. "You will have several men in your life," she told me. "And you will have three different husbands."

"Let's go," one of my friends said. "This is stupid."

There was no divorce in China at that time. Maybe you separated, but there was no way to get remarried. It just seemed ridiculous to us. When I told my mother about it, she said, "You're not going anywhere, little girl." She said I was going to stay right there and have lots of grandchildren for her and my father. This was before they imposed the one-child limit in China.

It cost ten cents to go to that fortune teller, a lot of money back then. I used money I got from recycling to go there. Afterward, I felt like I'd wasted my money and time. There were cheaper ones, but my friend had wanted to go there, because she said that old woman was the best.

My mother called me back to tell me that the fortune teller had looked at Tony's picture and said he was a very generous man who would be a lot of help in my life and that he was a good man with a very good heart. I already knew this, but how did that fortune teller know, just by looking at his picture?

I found myself wishing that my father's father was alive. He'd been a famous fortune teller. I would ask him what I was supposed to do about my husband, Tony, and my life. He would have had answers for me that nobody else would have.

Three weeks passed, and I had not talked to my boss at the antiques company once. Then he called and said he needed me to come to work the next day. On my way there, I had an accident in the little blue Escort I'd just gotten. The accident was my fault. I was just so depressed and not focused on what I was doing.

An ambulance took me to the hospital, and they towed my car. I was in the hospital for two days. Luckily, I had already dropped Yangyang off at daycare, and she was with Tony while I was in the hospital. I lost my job at the antiques company. I lost my car. I was completely broken again. I decided, lying in that hospital bed, that this was not the way my life was going to be. I needed to forget about Lu and start concentrating on Yangyang. I needed to figure out exactly how I was going to make her life as good as it could be. I knew when I left the hospital that she was my only concern. But I still wasn't even sure how I was going to legally keep her in America.

After I got out of the hospital, just a few days went by before I got another call from my husband's girlfriend. It seems she was tired of him. He had no work visa; he had no money. She said she was tired of paying for everything and asked if she could send him back to Houston. She told me he was still in love with me. I told her to put Lu on the phone—if he could tell me he was sorry and that he truly loved me, then maybe I would take him back. I heard her yelling at him to get on the phone. She told him that all he had to do was say he was sorry, and he could go home to his wife and baby. I waited for him to come to the phone and say something, but he never did. I hung up and decided to file for a divorce.

XIII: Red Ink

I called my attorney the next day and got the paperwork started. He told me the only way he could guarantee that I'd be able to stay in America with my child was if I got married again to an American citizen. I told him I'd have to take a risk, because I did not want to be married to Lu anymore.

Tony is Muslim, and in his religion there was no way he could be with a married woman. He had already asked me to marry him, when I first met him. That was when I told him about my husband and child in China. At this point, we had kissed, but we had never spent the night together. We weren't dating. As soon as I told him I'd sent the divorce papers to my husband, he said, "That's it. We're getting married."

I wasn't sure about anything anymore, so I agreed. I knew I cared about Tony, but I wasn't even divorced from Lu yet.

When Lu got the divorce papers, he called to say he wanted to go back to China with Yangyang. "There's no way you're taking Yangyang anywhere," I told him.

"She's my daughter too," Lu said, with the most anger I'd ever heard in his voice.

"If you stay in America when you get your visa straightened out, and you get a stable place to stay," I told him as sternly as possible, "then you can come get her anytime you want. But she's staying with me."

"I'm not sure I'm going to stay in America. I might go back to China," he told me. "But I don't want to be that far away from her."

"Why don't you move to Houston?" I asked.

He laughed at me. "There's no way I'm going to live in the same town as you while you're with another man."

At that point, he still had a chance to save our marriage. I guess he was still just too full of pride. He did stay in America, though. He lives in Rolland Heights, California, to this day. He sees Yangyang regularly.

He thought our marriage was over, but the truth is, he could have saved it with very little effort. He seemed to not even try. I've wondered a thousand times why he didn't say he wanted to take me and Yangyang back to China. I never would have gone with him, but it would have made me feel a lot better if he had tried.

I realized I was going to marry Tony soon, and no one in my family had ever met him. We'd set a date for Thanksgiving, and it was now the end of September. I'd called my parents to tell them, and I could tell they were upset. They were upset because they knew they wouldn't be here, and because I wasn't marrying a Chinese man. They couldn't even talk to Tony; he doesn't speak any Chinese. They weren't sure how he would treat Yangyang and me. But mostly they were upset because I'd gotten divorced in the first place.

My aunt called from Dallas several times, asking me to visit. So I decided I'd get Tony to take me; at least they'd be able to meet him. My aunt is my father's sister, so I guess that was the next best thing to having Tony meet my father. They were the only family I had in America at that time. Plus, my grandmother was there. She'd always been a wise lady. Tony agreed to drive me to Dallas for the weekend, but the trip didn't go my way at all.

I could tell right away that they didn't like Tony, even though he brought a big potted plant as a gift. My aunt did say thank you, but she sounded like someone had handed her a big dead fish. Of course, the whole time we were there, she was asking Tony to fix all kinds of things around her house.

She said so many rude things right in front of him. First, she started the whole thing again about my moving to Dallas to live with them. Then she asked me if I was looking for a father—Tony is ten years older than I am. I couldn't believe it when she said I could do better by picking someone up off the street. I know my aunt meant well, though. I know she was trying to look out for my best interests. I love my aunt, and that's just the way she is.

My aunt has always thought of herself as upper class and well-to-do. They do have a nice lifestyle, but they aren't rich. They just didn't like him; I don't know why. My aunt is a good woman, though. She's helped me a lot in my life. There's always somebody in your family who thinks that nobody is good enough for you. She hadn't wanted me to marry Lu, either. She told me that my goal was to come to America and live with them. She had my whole life planned out for me.

On the way back to Houston, I did a lot of thinking. I knew I could still call this marriage off. Believe it or not, I still hoped I'd hear from Lu. I remembered when I first got married back in China. It was such a great celebration. I thought about when Yangyang was first born, how happy the family was. I started crying, and Tony asked me what was wrong. I told him that everything seemed wrong.

"No. Everything is not wrong. I love you," he said. "I'm going to help you and your baby get your green cards, and we're going to bring your parents here and get their green cards too." He hugged me and told me that together we were going to make everything right. He said he'd take care of my daughter and my parents like they were his own.

By the time we got back to Houston, I felt a lot better about my decision to marry this man. He'd been there for me through some of my worst times and had never failed me. I knew he was an honest man, and I knew he was good with Yangyang. I felt I could trust him. My mother had even told me that the fortune teller had nothing but good things to say about Tony.

On November 27, 1997, we were married. It was Thanksgiving Day. I had invited my aunt, my uncle, and my grandmother, but they didn't come. I wasn't that surprised. One of my girlfriends was there, and a couple of Tony's friends were there. I think I cried for most of the day, out of sadness. I couldn't believe I had divorced Yangyang's father so fast, and now I was marrying this man. I kept asking myself, *Am I doing the right thing?*

I wasn't in a white wedding dress. I was dressed in a traditional blue Chinese Qipao dress. We were married at the house of a friend of Tony's who is a Hajji. He's qualified in the Muslim community to perform weddings. We were married in a Muslim ceremony. There were wild turkeys in the backyard. Yangyang had a great time chasing them. That was the only thing I laughed at all day.

During the ceremony, the Hajji told me that, in the Muslim tradition, I had a right to ask my husband for anything I wanted. "Only up to one million dollars though," he said with a laugh.

"I need a new car," I told him.

"In what price range would you like this car?" he asked.

Since it was just an old tradition and a chance to make a wish, I said, "Forty to fifty thousand dollars."

You know, it took him a while, but Tony did finally get me a new car. It was a 2004 Volvo S40 with zero miles. That was a good day.

When it came time to eat, I had a real problem. They had prepared a formal Iranian dinner, to be served on a huge cloth spread out on a rug. Everyone sat around the rug on the floor. But my Qipao dress was tight and slit up the side. That's the way they're made. At a Chinese wedding, no one sits down. I couldn't sit with my legs crossed like everyone else. I had to sit with both legs off to one side. Even sitting like this, my dress kept sliding up, showing my legs. Tony kept reaching over and pulling it back down.

The food was fantastic, but there were no forks or spoons—not even chopsticks! Everyone ate with their hands. I felt so awkward and uncomfortable. I kept going to the restroom to cry. I believed Tony was a good man, but I wasn't sure how well I knew him. I missed Lu and my parents so much. When Lu and I got married, it was a huge celebration with both families. This time, I felt alone on my wedding day. It was rough. Life can be rough and confusing. The whole day was a culture shock for me.

I was still kind of sick, I was broke, and I wasn't working. I'd tried to get food stamps and a medical card for Yangyang and me, but I'd been denied since I had no green card. I wasn't an American citizen yet, so I wasn't entitled to any of the benefits that come with citizenship. My daughter and I were in limbo.

I learned a lot about Iranian culture that day.

"You're not supposed to eat pork, but I'm very sure you'll be a part-time Muslim," the Hajji told me. "You won't eat pork when you're with your husband, but when you're with your friends, I'm sure you will." He was a very funny man. But he was right—I love pork. "I know you feel strange right now," he said, "but later on, you'll get used to it."

The Hajji gave me a book explaining how a Muslim woman is supposed to cover her hair and how she is supposed to pray. He also told me about fasting. He told me about a lot of things I'd never dealt with before. It was intimidating, to say the least.

It was really weird when everyone got up to go and pray. Muslims do this five times a day. I'd never experienced anything like it. The Hajji's wife took me to one of the bedrooms to show me how to pray. First, she covered me from head to toe, with only my face showing. "You're not supposed to show any hair at all," she said, "or any skin at all—only your face."

That was my first and last time praying.

In China, when I was growing up, there was no religion at all. Our leader, Mao, had done away with all churches and temples. There were religious movements, but they were all underground. When I came to America, I went to a church. I knew it was a sacred place, and I wanted to have that experience. Today, I understand what Mao Zedong meant: organized religion can be a very dangerous thing. It seems to me that most of the religions in America are geared toward profit.

Since I was now married to Tony, we decided he would let his apartment go, and move into the townhouse with us. It seemed like the most convenient thing to do. I went straight to my attorney to start the process of getting green cards for my daughter and me. I was still so sad, crying all the time. Tony was working, but I had no work. When I applied for our green cards, I applied for food stamps and a medical cards right away. I didn't get the food stamps, but I did get the medical cards.

When Tony came home from work each day, I would be crying and listening to Chinese music. Finally, he said something had to change. He threw away all my Chinese CDs, but he was my husband now, and I had to respect his wishes.

"We're moving out of this house," he said, "so we can start all over again somewhere new, with all new memories." After some thought, I decided he was right. It was time for me to face reality, for my daughter, for myself, and for our future. I needed to move on and realize that I was in a new marriage now. I needed to be strong for Yangyang. I needed to accept that her father had made his choice.

We put the house up for sale and started looking for a new house to live in. We also started thinking about what kind of new business we could start. When we found the new house, we still had not sold the townhouse, so we decided to rent it out instead. We still have it as a rental property, even now.

My parents had been talking to me regularly through all of this. They knew my whole situation and were very worried about Yangyang and me. They kept saying they missed her and that I should send her to stay with them until I got everything situated. They knew Tony was the only one making any money, and they knew we were moving into a new house. They also knew we were about to start a new business. I told them that as soon as my attorney said it was okay for us to travel back to China, I would bring Yangyang over.

Tony and I talked a lot about different businesses. We didn't have much money, and we knew the best way to make money was to be in business for ourselves. Tony still had his limo business, but it made barely enough to pay the bills. Every evening, we looked through the Houston *Chronicle*'s business section and talked about what we planned to do.

One evening, I saw a check-cashing business for sale. I noticed it because it was the cheapest business I'd seen for sale. I didn't even know what a check-cashing business was; I'd been in the United States for less than two years and had never even written a check. Everything in China was done with cash. My job at the antiques place paid cash; even the dentist's office paid cash.

I showed the ad to Tony. He knew what a check-cashing business was but had no idea how to run one. It cost only fifteen thousand dollars. Between the two of us, we could borrow ten thousand dollars. We called and explained our situation, and they said come to their store so we could talk about it. We ended up paying nine thousand dollars for the business and one thousand dollars for the first month's rent on the location. It took a lot of negotiating; I know the old couple didn't make any money from the deal. They probably even lost a little. I want to thank them for helping a new couple get a foothold in life.

Neither of us knew anything about running this business. For instance, I didn't know that the checks had to be cleared by the bank; or that people would write a check when they had no money at all; or, even worse, that the check might be stolen. In the first month alone, I accepted over ten thousand dollars in bad checks at my store.

Sometimes it can take up to ten days for banks to clear the checks, and by that point, all our money would be out the door. The bank would tell us we weren't going to get a large portion of it back. We borrowed money from friends and relatives, basically borrowing from Peter to pay Paul, as they say. Things were tight, and the business situation was very frustrating.

I decided I'd send Yangyang back to China to stay with my parents for a little while, but I would stay in America. I needed to concentrate on my new business. This was a very hard decision. It seemed like we'd just been reunited. I thought about it for days before deciding, but I felt it would be best for her. I was working all the time, and our business was losing money.

I needed to turn things around soon. Tony was spending all his time with his limo service, so I knew it was up to me.

When Yangyang left, I decided that when she came back home, she'd have a whole new set of furniture in her room at our new house. She was only three and a half years old, but I was already treating her like a little adult. She's always been my best friend. I told my parents that I wasn't sure how long they could keep her. I wasn't sure how long I could stand being away from her. I told them no longer than six months. I have a cousin, living in Dallas, his name is Sheng. I knew that he was going back to China for a visit soon. I called him and asked if he would take her to my parents. I told him that they were going to take care of her for a while. So I can get my new business out of the red. He agreed and then she was gone again.

This time it was different; I knew she was coming back. My attorney had told me that as soon as I received my green card, I could invite my parents to come and live in America with us. I had a goal for myself and my family, and nothing was going to stop me. I started working seven days a week again. I missed Yangyang very much, but I had no time for sadness. I was totally focused on the task at hand.

I realized that America was full of hustlers. When people saw that I was Chinese and couldn't speak good English, I became a mark. But I decided I wasn't going to put up with it. I knew I had to learn about the hustlers. I had to learn to read their faces and their attitudes. It was Psychology 101.

I was probably a bitch to some of my customers at that time, and I want to say I'm sorry. I got so used to people trying to cheat me; it was a daily occurrence. Then, one day, I was arguing with a man about the amount of money I'd handed him, when all at once I realized it was my mistake. I'd shorted him twenty dollars. I was so embarrassed, because I'd been sure I was in the right. I handed the man his twenty dollars and apologized with a red face.

Some of them understood and became regulars, though. The man I just described is still a customer to this day. I had to explain that there was a new sheriff in town, and if they wanted my location to stay open, they were going to have to work with me, not against me. I learned more legal stuff than I ever thought I'd know. I talked to so many detectives and attorneys. I learned all about the banks' procedures. It was quite a learning experience.

We got settled in the new house, and the business slowly started to come together. I added a gift shop, since I had a little bit of extra room.

I sold toys, baby clothes, and other odds and ends. We still barely broke even the first year, but we did manage to pay back everyone who had lent us money, with interest. I learned so much about American culture that first year in business for myself. There is no culture—everyone is such an individual. I still don't know if this is a good thing or a bad thing. I just know it's a weird thing.

If I ran a check-cashing business in China, I'd be dealing with Chinese all day. But in America, I was dealing with Hispanics, whites, Pakistanis, Africans, African Americans, and any Asian culture you can think of. I was dealing with people from all over the world. It doesn't matter where you're from, though. You either have a good heart or you don't. I've met some great people from every corner of this planet.

It was so hard letting Yangyang go to stay with my parents in China. I called her as soon as I knew she was with them. My mother was very surprised, saying she couldn't talk to Yangyang because she spoke only English now. "Tell me what my grandchild is saying to me," my mother said. I told her to put Yangyang on the phone. She was saying *bird* and *fish*, because my parents had a pet bird and a goldfish. Right away, I heard my mother telling Yangyang how to say the words in Chinese.

My plan was to have my parents come with her back to America for a visit. Yangyang had gone to China with my cousin, who was now back in America. Things didn't go as planned, however. It had been six months since I'd seen her, but my parents couldn't get visas. They tried twice and failed both times. This meant they'd traveled all the way to Beijing and back home again twice, just to be denied. My father was very upset and didn't know what to do.

Tony and I decided to go to China and bring Yangyang back ourselves. Tony said that since we were going to be landing in Beijing, we would see if we could get my parents' visas cleared.

The plane trip to China seemed to take forever. It was very emotional for me. Not only had I not seen my daughter in six months, but I had also not seen my parents or my country for three years. When I left China, I didn't know how long I'd be gone, or if I'd ever return. When I saw the Chinese flag flying at the airport, I was overcome with gratitude and clarity. I understood what my country meant to me. It could be the coldest winter, but, even now, something about China makes me feel warm and safe. At least I know that every person there is equally loved and important.

When I saw my parents at the airport, and they saw their new son-in-law for the first time, it was hard. I thought about the good times when I was young, living in Kaifeng with my mother. I hugged my mother and father, crying. My mother held Yangyang, who was also crying. Tony must have felt as out of place as I had at our wedding. At least everyone at our wedding spoke English. Tony could not even speak with my parents. Even Yangyang was now speaking only Chinese.

When we left Beijing, we went to Kaifeng, where my relatives had planned a big celebration for me and my new husband. This got very awkward. Tony doesn't drink alcohol, but that's a big part of the celebration. I tried to tell them that he's Muslim, and in the Muslim religion, they do not drink alcohol. My family insisted that he have one drink. Tony proceeded to get drunk. I know he didn't mean to, but later he told me it was the first time he'd ever drunk alcohol. I thought it was hilariously funny.

My parents told me how Yangyang had won a competition in a children's talent show in Zhengzhou City. She sang "Twinkle, Twinkle, Little Star," and everyone was impressed with the cute little Chinese girl singing in English. It turns out that she taught several other children how to sing "Twinkle, Twinkle, Little Star" in English as well. My father had been teaching her Tai Chi too. She had forgotten all other English and was speaking only Chinese. She looked at Tony and said *Daddy* and started talking to him in Chinese. Tony told her not to worry, she'd learn English again in no time.

Before we traveled to China, I'd told my parents to bring their documents so that we could go with them to the American Embassy while we were in Beijing and try to get their visas again. But they didn't bring their documents. My father said they were not going through the humiliation of being turned down again. I was disappointed, but I understood. When I was turned down for a student visa, I'd had the same feeling. It was humiliating. Luckily, I got to America through the Chinese government. I didn't have to go through the American Embassy.

Since my parents hadn't brought their papers, we didn't stay in Beijing; we took the train back to Zhengzhou the same day. All of the main train lines had been updated since I'd lived in China. I was amazed at how fast the train was. The trip took about a quarter of the time it used to take.

Not many foreigners traveled through China, especially by train. Everyone gathered around Tony, asking me to translate questions and answers for them. They wanted to know everything about America. They were surprised to see a Chinese woman married to an American man. Even though Tony has an Iranian accent, they didn't know; they all thought he was American.

When we arrived in Zhengzhou, it was late. Tony and I were very tired from traveling. I just wanted to go to my parents' house and sleep. But there was a law in China that said foreigners were not allowed to stay in residential housing while visiting China.

"You and your new husband will have to stay at a hotel tonight," my father told me.

"Tony is family now. He's your new son-in-law," I said. "We came all the way from America to see you."

"Just for tonight," my father said. "We'll deal with it in the morning."

"Nobody is going to know who's staying at your house," I told him.

"You can stay," my father said, "but he'll have to go to the proper office to get a permit to allow him to stay in my house."

Maybe my father was just being that way because Tony is not Chinese. I decided I'd just go with Tony to the Henan International Hotel. Foreigners were allowed to stay only in the International Hotels. When we got to the hotel, we were asked for our marriage license, which we did not have with us; I'd forgotten to bring it. This caused another problem. My father called a friend who managed a Muslim hotel. Since Tony is Muslim, we were able to stay there in the same room without showing a marriage license.

The whole experience was a little overwhelming for Tony, and for me too, really. My mother insisted that Yangyang stay with her and my father for the night. She said she could tell I was too tired to take care of her. I was tired, but I wanted her to stay with me. I let her go, though, because I knew that soon my parents would be missing her like I had been all that time.

We checked into the room, and both of us went to sleep almost immediately. I've never been so tired. My body seemed to weigh a ton. I'd hardly slept at all in the past four days. The next morning, I woke up to Yangyang standing beside the bed saying, "Momma." I thought I was dreaming again. I always had a dream in which she called me, but when I woke up, she was never there.

This time she was there, along with my father, my mother, and one of the hotel staff. It was afternoon. My mother said they'd tried to call our room several times and had knocked on the door with no answer. She'd finally gotten the hotel staff to open the door.

Tony and I were both sick, running high fevers. I could hardly open my eyes; there was no way I could get out of bed. Since my mother is a doctor, she went to her clinic and came back with IVs for both of us. We were terribly dehydrated.

"Congratulations! I got you a permit this morning," my father said. "Now both of you can stay at my house." Then he said, "Now I'm going to see how long you can stay at the hotel here, because neither one of you is going anywhere right now."

Neither Tony nor I got out of the bed for the next two days except to use the bathroom. On the third day, my father came and wanted to take us around the city. I was so weak I just couldn't do it. Tony was feeling better, so they went without me.

My father showed Tony my old school and the house we used to live in. Basically, he showed him all the places where I grew up. My father took him all around town on his motorcycle. Tony thought that was great. I don't know how they communicated, since Tony doesn't understand Chinese and my father speaks no English, but Tony and my father have always gotten along great.

I wasn't just physically sick; I was also mentally sick. I was completely drained of all my energy. I felt like I'd been fighting a constant battle for the past four years. I hadn't realized how much I'd missed China and my parents. All I'd been thinking about was Yangyang and how to get her to America with me. Now I was home, with all the memories of first meeting her father, then marrying him, and her birth. It was all too much. I was at home, where I felt safe, and I think I just collapsed.

It took me a few more days to start feeling good again. Each time my mother brought Yangyang to see me, I felt stronger. I knew I'd be taking her back to America with me soon, where we would start a new life. No one was ever going to take my daughter away from me. I never wanted to be without her again.

We were in China for three weeks, and because I was feeling so poorly, I didn't see any of my friends or old classmates. I did see family, though. My family is so great; everyone got together and threw a mock wedding for Tony and me. I couldn't believe it. It was really special.

We spent the first two weeks in Henan Province, running around visiting family—after I started feeling better, of course. The third week, we went to Beijing with my parents to try to get visas for them. Once again, my mother and father were full of pride and trying to be stubborn about the whole thing. I told them that if they wanted to visit me and Yangyang in America, then they had to go to the American Embassy with us.

When we first arrived in Beijing, Tony went straight to the American Embassy to ask why his in-laws were being denied visas to visit him and his new wife in America. Tony is an American citizen, so he could go straight to the embassy and speak with someone in charge without an appointment. Since we are all Chinese, we would have had to make an appointment, pay a fee, and come back another day to wait in line. He was able to step around all of that. We still had to pay a fee, and my parents still had to stand in line the next day for their appointment. But they got an appointment right away and also had a recommendation from an American citizen, which can make all the difference in the world.

We were leaving the day of my parents' appointment, so we got a taxi early the next morning and dropped them off at the embassy. It was very emotional; we didn't know if they would get visas or not. We knew the chances were better, but still. I knew I wasn't coming back to China for a long time, and now I was taking Yangyang with me. I felt so bad leaving my parents there to stand in that long line. Just before we boarded the plane, I got a phone call from them saying that they'd been granted visas. We were all so relieved.

XIV: Together Again

This time, when I went back to America, things were a lot different. I wasn't weak and sad like before. I had Yangyang with me, and I knew my parents were coming to visit for at least six months. I'd promised Yangyang that when she came back I'd have all new furniture in her room, and I did.

I know it didn't make any difference to her, since she was not quite four years old, but it made a lot of difference to me. I'm one of those people who like to set goals. Once I've set the goal, I have to achieve it, one way or another. I've always been that way, probably because of my father. I just felt like I needed to do something for her. I felt so guilty for sending her back to China without me.

The day after we got back, Yangyang had to test for preschool registration, because she was from China and spoke two languages. My friend had just registered her daughter the year before and told me what type of questions they would ask. On the flight home, I started teaching her everything I could. I started speaking only English to her so that she'd get familiar with it again. I started getting her to count from one to twenty in English and tell me what different colors and animals were. She thought it was all a fun game. I kept thinking, *I just hope she passes.*

When I first knew I was going to live in America, I had thought about the fact that my name was Yanyan, how were people in America going to react. Mr. Wishnow had taken care of that for me. Everyone knew me as Grace. Now I felt like my daughter should do the same. I asked her if she wanted to change her name so that she'd have an English name when she went to school. Again, she thought it was big fun.

We went to a bookstore, where I picked up a name book. I started reading the names aloud. As soon as I said "Yvonne," she said, "Yes,

Yvonne. I like that name." That became her new name. Now I was Grace, and she was Yvonne. I didn't change my name legally until I became an American citizen. She has never changed her name legally to Yvonne, but everyone has always called her Yvonne. Except the family. The family still calls her Yangyang.

When I took her to the test, the teacher said she'd have to start with the program for English as a second language. She also told me that since Yvonne was not quite four years old, she could wait for one more year before registering. I asked Yvonne if she wanted to start school now or wait until next year. She said she wanted to start now. She also told me she liked the school. She said it was bigger than her other school, and there were no babies. She really liked the orange school buses and the big playground. I was happy for her.

It was one more thing off my mind. Yvonne's school situation had been worrying me for a while. I knew she wasn't speaking English well, and I was worried about her adjusting to her new surroundings. She'd now changed her name to Yvonne. I told her to pay attention and be sure to listen. I was afraid she wouldn't respond when they called her Yvonne.

I don't know how she adjusted to all these things, but she did. In fact, she really didn't have many problems at all. It was just a big game to her, and she wanted to be the winner. Daycare was very expensive. We were really struggling at the time, trying to make the check-cashing business profitable. So I was glad she wanted to start preschool right away.

Then there was the problem with her immunization shots. It wasn't good enough that she'd already had them in China. Now I had to put her through that again. More shots, more money—I felt like everything was changing for her too fast. Every day it was something, and she was so little. She cried so loudly when the doctor gave her the shots that my heart shook.

My next big problem was that Yvonne's new school required a uniform. When we went to buy her one, they were all too big. Even the smallest skirt they had wouldn't fit her little waist; she was so tiny. I bought the smallest they had and altered them at home to make them fit.

On her first day of school, I pinned a big pink badge on her shirt with my phone number, our home address, her name, her teacher's name, and anything else I could think of to keep my little girl from getting lost. She was speaking English a little better, but she'd just arrived from China three days earlier, and I felt like I was putting her out in the world all by herself.

I told the bus driver to make sure he saw her go to her teacher and to make sure he got her back home safely. I just kept thinking, *I hope she's all right.* I'm still always thinking the same thing.

Once you have a child, your life is not your own anymore. It doesn't matter what I do or plan; she's always part of it. Kids always grow up and break your heart. They're never going to be exactly how you want them to be. They can be so ungrateful at times, but you wouldn't trade them for all the riches in the world. I'm so proud of my daughter and all the things she has overcome. In a lot of ways, I think she's a lot stronger than I am.

"What did you learn in school today, Yvonne?" I asked her in English when she came home the first day.

"Nothing. We played all day," she said.

"Did you understand your teachers when they were talking to you?" I asked.

"Yes, Mom, I understand everything," she said. But I barely understood what she was saying to me.

"Did they send any homework with you?" I asked.

"What is that?" she asked me with a stunned look on her face.

I looked in her book bag, and she did have homework. I don't think she understood anything. She was speaking English better than she understood it. It was funny at first to listen to her. She would say things even though she had no idea how to say them properly. Within a few weeks, though, she started to speak and understand English pretty well, and I started getting good reports from her teachers at school.

Just after her fourth birthday, I took her to the mall, where there was an ice rink. When she saw everyone skating, she got really excited. I asked her if she wanted to try, and she said yes. The first thing she did was fall down and start crying. She didn't like ice skating very much.

I have a friend with two daughters who study dance. When they had a dance recital, she got tickets for Yvonne and me. Yvonne loved to dance, so I thought it would be great for her. After the show, they mentioned that they were recruiting new students four years old and up. I asked Yvonne if she wanted to join, and she said yes. I could tell by the look on her face that she wanted to do it more than anything, so we signed her up. My daughter has been a professionally trained dancer ever since. She's studied so many styles of dance and done so many performances that I can't even list them all.

I had so much going on. I was busy with my business and taking care of Yvonne—she was in school for only four hours each day. Now I also had to take her to dance classes three times a week. I had a new husband and a new house to deal with. I was a little overwhelmed and was starting to feel rundown.

I called my parents to ask when they would be coming to visit. They both had their own private businesses in China. "Your granddaughter misses you very much," I told them.

They said they needed a little more time to get everything arranged properly. They told me they'd be in Houston by the end of November. That meant I wouldn't see my parents for another month. I had one black-and-white TV and only regular cable. My goal was to have two TVs and the Chinese network hooked up before my parents arrived. My parents don't speak any English and understood very little at the time. Plus, I knew they'd want to know what was going on back home while they were here.

I did have the Chinese network when they arrived. I had bought a nineteen-inch color TV for the living room, and I put the smaller black-and-white TV in Yvonne's room. That way, I thought she could watch cartoons and learn English better. She loved watching cartoons, and she started drawing the characters. She was good at it too. When I went to parent/teacher night at her school, I saw that her teacher had Yvonne's drawings hanging all around the classroom. Her teacher kept bragging about how good an artist she was.

I was so relieved when my parents arrived. It was great seeing them again. My mother is always such a fantastic help around the house, and she loves spending time with Yvonne. I always feel stronger when my father is around. He started helping me with my business, even though they'd just arrived earlier that day.

"Dad, aren't you tired?" I asked him. It was almost midnight. "Mom went to sleep over an hour ago."

"Don't you have to open your business tomorrow?" he asked.

"Yes," I told him, "but you can stay here and rest."

"No, wake me in the morning," he told me. "I want to go with you. Now give me a breakdown of what it is you do." My father sat there with me, going over business plans, until about two in the morning. He had some very good ideas and insisted on going with me the next morning.

I felt like I could finally throw myself completely into the new check-cashing business. It wasn't really new anymore; we'd owned it for almost a year. But I was still barely breaking even. I could see that if I kept going, though, things would turn around. I'd started paying back some of the money we'd once again borrowed from friends and family, with interest. That was one thing I felt really good about.

I needed this business to work more than anything. I needed to be able to give my child a good life. I hadn't spoken to my parents about it yet, but I also wanted them to stay in America. They didn't know that we had no money and that we had borrowed so much. My father would have wanted to kill me if he knew. Everything hinged on this business, so I was under a lot of pressure. I seem to always put myself in positions like that.

In my father's eyes, though, everything was great. He loved the business we'd started. "This is one of the best things you've done in your life, Yanyan," he told me that first day as we closed the shop.

I decided to take my parents to Yvonne's school, where they had an English-language program for adults. At the same time, I started teaching them to drive. This was not easy; my parents had never driven a car before. My father had driven a motorcycle in China, but that was totally different from driving a car in America. My mother was driving okay, so Tony decided he'd help my father.

It was very hard for my parents. They held high positions in China and had good educations. "Now your father and I feel like we're dumb and uneducated," my mother said. "We can't read or write or speak properly."

"It's okay. I felt the same way when I first came to America," I told her. "But you and dad will find your places here."

And they have.

Tony and I bought a cheap used car for my parents to drive. This was great until my father crashed it into a tree right in front of our house. He felt so bad about it. He did, however, get his license right away, which was more than I could say for my mother. She took the driving test six times before passing. Every time she went, the same fat woman gave her the driving test.

My mother said that every time the woman sat down in the passenger seat, the whole car leaned to that side. "I get too nervous, Yanyan," my mother told me. "Every time I see that fat woman coming, I know I'm not going to pass." Plus, she said she couldn't understand the woman's English. Finally, on her sixth try, she had a different instructor, and she passed.

When we were looking for a house to live in, I almost bought one in Chinatown. Considering Tony, I decided to buy just outside of Chinatown. Now I was glad I did, because my parents started going to Chinatown just about every day. Finally, my father was so bored, he said he needed to do something with himself.

I had a friend who ran a Tai Chi school, and I asked if I could rent space from him for my father to teach ballroom dancing. He agreed, and it worked out great; the friend taught during the day, and my father held his school at night. My father is still in the same building to this day. He has his own bigger space now, where he teaches ballroom dancing and Kung Fu. He and my mother have both been very successful in America.

Yvonne has learned ballroom dancing, Tai Chi, and Kung Fu from her grandfather. I think that's just great. She's won competitions in all these things. Three years in a row, she was at the top of her class in ballroom dancing for her age group. It seems like she's always been on stage. She loves to perform, no matter what she's doing. Dancing, acting, modeling, Kung Fu—it's all the same to her.

At one of her beginning dance performances, she was the leader, because she could memorize the moves very well and was good at entertaining the crowd. I was so impressed with her, she was only five years old. Everyone was in a line, with their hands on one another's shoulders, and she was leading. Her teacher motioned for her to leave the stage, but Yvonne was so into the crowd and was enjoying her dance so much that she proceeded to leave the stage the wrong way. Some of the girls stayed with her, while others split off toward the teacher. Several girls stayed on the stage, confused, not knowing what to do. The audience started laughing. Yvonne looked back and saw what had happened. She was so upset that she started to cry. I was laughing and crying at the same time; I felt so bad for her. The girls who were left on stage started crying. This was the first of many stage disasters for her.

By the time she was four and a half, she had become quite a little character. She was always putting on different costumes and makeup and acting like a little star around the house. I thought this child was going to be a handful, and she has been.

Her English started to get a lot better, and she was speaking Chinese with my parents all the time. She was actually translating for my father and his students at his dance studio. Everything was starting to gel. My business was getting better, and I had paid back everything we'd borrowed.

My parents got a six-month extension on their visas, and they seemed very happy with their new dance studio. They had a lot of students. When my father started the dance studio, three other studios in the area were teaching ballroom dancing. One by one, over time, they closed. My father is the only one there now.

The first time I mentioned the idea of staying in America to my parents was when they got extensions on their visas. My father told me that eventually they'd have to go back to China. I knew I was pushing my luck. In my wildest dreams, I'd never thought I'd be living in America with my little girl and my parents for this long. I thought that if I could stay here with her and visit them sometimes, that should be enough. But it wasn't. I wanted them to stay here and live in America with me and their granddaughter.

Their only problem was that they both still had businesses in China. They were supposed to renew their business licenses in person each year, but they'd managed to get around this so far. My mother wouldn't even consider coming to America until my grandparents had passed away. Both of my parents still have brothers and sisters living in China. I'm really close to some of them, almost like I'm their own child.

When Yvonne turned five, it was a big deal. All her previous birthdays had kind of just slipped by, because our lives had been so crazy—she was in China while I was in America, or my parents were in China while she and I were in America. Now the whole family was together. Plus, Tony's family and friends were there, and Yvonne's friends from school came. It was a huge birthday celebration. After it was over, she was really tired, so I put her to sleep. I remember the look on her face while I was watching her sleeping. She was so happy and so beautiful, with her little baby face. I've always loved watching her sleep.

I was working hard every day for a lot of hours, and time just flew by. The next thing I knew, my parents' visas were running out again. I used the same excuses to keep them here, saying I was running my own business, Yvonne was still young, and I needed them here to help me with her. I could have afforded to pay for daycare at that time, but I just didn't want my parents to leave. Once again, I asked them about just staying here. I told them I could talk to my attorney and start the paperwork. My father said they'd stay for another six months. He said maybe by then my business would be more stable.

My business was already turning around, but I didn't want them to know that. I didn't want them to go back to China. I wanted them to stay here with us so that they could watch their granddaughter grow up and be part of her life.

There was a lot of stress in my marriage at this time. I have to say, I know Tony loves me. We had hardly any time alone, and my parents were living with us for free. All I talked about was Yvonne. People were telling him I'd married him only to get my citizenship and to bring my parents and child here. When he told me this, I didn't know what to say. I'd been so confused when we got married that I had to think about it. But over time, I've realized that I married him because he's a good person and a responsible husband with a big heart.

Just after Yvonne turned six, we were invited to her school for open-house night. I'd seen how good she was at drawing at home, but I had no idea how good she actually was. In her class, she was using different materials, and painting, and all of it was really good. I saw a picture she'd drawn of our house with the car and the flowers and trees in our front yard, with all of us standing there, even all the dogs. We had a lot of dogs. We have four dogs now; we're dog people. The point is, it looked just like our house and us. She'd drawn this picture for a competition at her school and had won first place.

When we got home, I asked her if she'd like to go to art school, and she said yes. I took her to the Xinsheng Art School, because I knew a famous Chinese artist was teaching there. She took to oil painting right away. I don't know what it is; she just has a golden touch. She started winning awards in her art school. Later, her teacher took one of her paintings to a competition covering all of Houston, and she won first place there too. My daughter is so talented. Whatever she does, she seems to excel at it.

She was now in first grade, and when they asked her at school what she wanted to be when she grew up, she said, "A star." I thought, *Oh, man, here we go*. She was like a little star, though. She still is.

A lot of things happened that year. My parents' visas were running out once again. This time, I knew my parents didn't want to leave, either. They'd been in America for a year and a half now. The dance studio was very successful; they had over three hundred students, and none of their students wanted them to leave. Plus, my father had become an editor for a major Chinese newspaper. Finally, they decided to stay. I started the paperwork right away to get them their green cards. When I walked out of the attorney's office, I was laughing to myself with joy. I just wanted to dance right there in the street.

XV: Disaster in America

Everything seemed to be falling into place. I was living my American dream. Then, all of a sudden, it was September 11, 2001. That morning, Tony got up at 4:00 a.m. to pick up one of his regular clients. I was getting Yvonne ready for school when he called and told me not to go anywhere. "Turn on the TV," he said. "Something terrible is happening in America."

When I did, I couldn't believe what I was seeing. I still can't believe it. I was crying and staring at the TV.

"What are you watching, Mommy?" Yvonne asked when she walked into the living room.

I didn't want her to see it, so I told her to get ready or she'd miss the bus.

We waited for the bus, but it never came. I wasn't sure what was going on, so I drove her to school. When we got there, there were no buses and no students, only a couple of police officers and teachers saying there would be no school due to the disaster. One of the officers told me to be careful and go straight home.

I noticed that there were no cars on the road. It was really scary and spooky. Of course, Tony came home early that day. The events of September 11, 2001, destroyed so many lives. I wouldn't want to compare Tony's loss to the losses in New York, but September 11, 2001, completely destroyed his limousine service. He never recovered after that. My business also slowed down. Even the attendance at my father's dance studio was low. I guess all of America was like that at the time. I know this destroyed a lot of the illusions I'd had about America. I think the whole thing was just terribly tragic and sad.

Shortly after that terrible day, I went to my store first thing one morning and found that I'd been robbed. Thieves had gotten into the store and broken into the ATM. They'd taken everything: all my money, all the lottery tickets, all the phone cards, even my computers. I was screwed, and good. I had to start all over again.

Without Tony's limo business, we were worse off than ever. I had to borrow money again, this time from the bank. Everything was awful. All I'd worked for was gone in the blink of an eye. It was horrible.

Tony was out of work and at home every day, so we found a location for a second check-cashing business. We rented space inside a convenience store. This was a much better location. Tony started running the first one, and I ran the new one. We were really short on money, though. It took a while to get everything turned around again.

It didn't help that Tony was robbed too. This time, they followed him home. It was a Saturday evening. The banks were closed, and there was no way we were leaving the money at that location anymore. He had no choice but to bring the money home. Luckily, they got only the small bills; he'd wrapped a one-hundred-dollar bill around all the small money and had the large bills in another pocket. Right when he got out of the car at the garage, they approached him.

They had a gun, they fired a shot, he gave them the money, and they ran. It was that fast. Yvonne was in the house sleeping with me at the time. It scared the hell out of me. That was it. I decided we'd sell the first location and move to a better neighborhood. Tony gave the police a description of the robbers, and we filed a police report, but the money was never recovered.

We rented out our house and bought a new house in Sugar Land, Texas, right outside of Houston, in a gated community. I felt a lot better. The school Yvonne was going to was much better, one of the top schools in Texas.

The only problem was that it was a lot farther for us to go to work. It was also a lot farther for my parents to get to Chinatown and their dance studio. After the move, my father started coming home less and less. He'd just stay at the dance studio all week. Yvonne also had to give up her art school. There was nobody to take her; my mother couldn't drive on the freeway. She still won't drive on the freeway.

One day, Yvonne was playing with the neighbor girl, who was a couple of years older. "Are you adopted?" the girl asked.

"No, I'm not," Yvonne said.

"What's your mother's last name?" the girl asked. "What's your father's last name? And what's your last name?"

When Yvonne told her, the girl said, "See? All of your last names are different. You're adopted."

Yvonne didn't know what to say. She ran home crying and started asking me why our last names were different. I had to explain the whole thing to her, but I don't think she really understood until her father came to visit her for the first time in four years.

That was a real shock for me. I hadn't known he was coming. He didn't call until he was in Houston. He told me what hotel he was staying at and asked me to bring Yvonne to see him.

When I told Tony that Lu was in town, I could see the surprise on his face. I told him Lu wanted me to bring Yvonne to see him. Tony seemed all right with the idea. I wasn't sure how I felt about it, but he is her father, so I took her to see him the next morning. It was a bittersweet reunion, to say the least. She was shy at first.

"This is your baba," I told her. "Your real baba."

She came around after a little while, and when she finally let him hug her, he started to cry. I felt so bad about the situation we were in. His daughter was growing up, and she didn't even know who he was. Finally, we were all crying. I've always wondered if she was crying just because we were crying; or if she was crying because she realized for the first time that her mother and father weren't together and that everything was not just as it should be in her family. Later, when we all calmed down, I could see the wheels turning in her little eight-year-old mind.

Lu took us to Target and bought her a CD player and a PlayStation II. I saw the way she was looking at him, and then she looked at me for approval. "It's okay; he's your baba," I told her. "He can buy you something. He loves you."

Then she started smiling. She kissed him on the cheek and said, "Thank you, Baba." I could tell that it made his day. His whole face lit up with a glow I hadn't seen since we first kissed.

"You don't have to say thank you to your baba," he told her.

It was another bittersweet moment for me. He stayed for one week. While he was there, he talked to me about helping him with the new business he'd started. From the way he talked to me, I felt like he wanted to see if there was anything left between us.

"I have a new husband, and we just bought a new house," I finally said.

We both stood there and cried for a few minutes. Then he looked at me and said, "I'm leaving tomorrow. I miss my daughter so much."

He was still living with that woman in Los Angles.

I could tell he was disappointed, but I knew there was no way I could trust him anymore. I still had feelings for him, I still loved him, but he'd hurt me so badly by bringing that woman into my home. I just couldn't find forgiveness in myself at that time.

The day he left, I had the same feeling I'd had when I saw him from the back of the bus, waving good-bye on his bicycle all those years ago. By now Yvonne knew she had a real father and a stepfather. It's never really bothered her; she has two daddies. She loves both of them very much, and Lu is a big part of her life.

Eventually we had the opportunity to buy the convenience store where we had our check-cashing business. Once again, we were blessed. The owners were retiring, and all we had to do was buy the merchandise; they gave us the store. Now we had our own convenience store, with Western Union check cashing. We named it Tony's Market.

It wasn't like we had the money to move into a new house, but I felt like we had no choice. Robbers with guns had been at my house, with my little girl right there in her bed—that wasn't going to do at all. That night, the police, the fire department, and the rescue squad all came, as well as the neighbors, because there had been a gunshot. It was all very embarrassing and terribly scary. I knew right away that we were moving, no matter what it took.

Believe me, it took a lot. We worked so hard on our new convenience store. We stayed open extra hours. I'm so glad my parents were there. I don't know what I would have done with Yvonne while we were spending so many hours at the store. There was no way we could afford daycare. Plus, we had a lot of extra expenses, because my parents were living with us. My mom never once hesitated to take care of Yvonne. I never let my parents know that our financial situation was that bad. They still don't know that we were that broke during that time.

Our days were hectic. My mom and I would drop Yvonne off at school, and then we would open the store and work until she got out of school. Then Tony would come to run the store, while my mother and I picked Yvonne up from school. Then I would drop her and my mother off at home and run back to the store so that I could get everything together to make a bank run.

Sometimes we'd make several trips to the bank in one day. We didn't have enough money to hire any employees, so we ran the store ourselves. Then I started getting followed on my trips to the bank. I started getting mysterious flat tires. It was all too much, so Tony and I decided to get guns. We went to a firing range and got certified. Now every time I went to the bank, I was carrying a gun. It was so crazy.

I can't tell you how many times we've been robbed. We eventually put up bulletproof glass. I can't believe no one has ever been shot or killed in that store. After 9/11, the economy was terrible. Robberies, shoplifting, people trying to sell us stolen goods—it was out of control. I couldn't handle it anymore. My mother didn't want to work at the store now that a gun was there. I couldn't believe that little ol' me, sweet as can be, was carrying a gun. I told Tony I couldn't do it anymore. I was scared all the time; it wasn't worth it.

That week, Hurricane Katrina hit. Thousands of people flooded into the Houston area from Louisiana, and the crime rate skyrocketed. There was a gunfight in front of our store, and someone was killed. That's when I quit. I told Tony that if we kept the store, he would have to run it. My mother and I couldn't work there anymore.

Almost every day, we found that someone had broken a window or cut a hole in the roof. It would always be for cigarettes, beer, or lottery tickets.

It seemed that every other night, the alarm at the store would go off, the police would call us, and Tony would have to rush to the store. We didn't have any money, but now he had to hire someone to work with him; plus he hired a security guard for the weekends. I don't know how he made it all work. He's still running that store. His son Amir works with him now. Amir has had shootouts with robbers several times; a recent incident was big news in Houston. I told him to just give them the money next time; it wasn't worth his life.

During the Katrina disaster, even my father's dance studio was robbed. Three guys with ski masks robbed him and all of his students in the middle of class. My father was devastated and so embarrassed.

It was a crazy time, but some good came from it. Yvonne met two kids at her school who were from New Orleans. She told me they needed help. They'd lost their parents to the storm, and they had no clothes except the ones on their backs. She donated a lot of her clothes, books, and toys to them. She even brought them home for dinner. She's always had a good heart and tries to help people. That's just one of the many things I love about her.

At one point during Katrina, they evacuated Houston, including Sugar Land. It wasn't a mandatory evacuation, and we chose to stay. Tony still opened the store every day, though we had no power for an entire week. Our store was in the news again, but this time it wasn't because we'd been robbed. It was because we were the only store open. Walmart, CVS, Kroger—all of them were closed. We helped a lot of people then, including ourselves. We sold out of everything we had. My mother and I worked with Tony during this time. In fact, we all worked there, even Yvonne. We all said to one another that if anything happened, at least we were all there together. It was the last time I worked at the store.

We were very busy, because everyone knew it was the only store in town that was open. With no power, the soda and beer were warm, but people didn't care; they bought everything. From that point on, our store has been very popular. People drive all the way across town just to come to our store. We have more regular customers than ever. We took a big risk when we decided to stay and open the store. We didn't make the decision lightly, but it worked out for the best in the end.

After that, the only work I did for the store was behind the scenes. I never ran the counter anymore, but I dealt with the vendors and the bank. When I went to the bank, however, our security guard went with me.

Now that I wasn't working at the store regularly, I had a lot more time with Yvonne. It was fantastic to have three generations at home, my mother, Yvonne, and me. We had so much fun together. We started helping my father with the dance studio. Yvonne started to become a really good dancer, and she was also winning Tai Chi competitions. I was the instructor for the yoga class. My mother helped my father teach students who were having problems with the dance moves. My mother and father are both great dancers. They used to win dance competitions in China. I told you that my mother used to do theater in China when she was younger.

XVI: Talent in the Family

One day, when Yvonne had just turned eight, she saw one of the neighborhood girls, about her age, all dressed up, going somewhere with her mother. "Where are you going dressed so nicely?" she asked.

"I'm competing in the Little Miss Houston Beauty Pageant," the girl said.

Yvonne ran to tell me about the pageant, saying she wanted to compete too. We jumped in the car and sped to a department store to find her an outfit for the competition, which was being held that day at the local mall. She took forever picking out the right outfit. She's always been very particular about this kind of thing.

"It's just a beauty pageant. Hurry up—we're going to be late," I told her.

"What's the point of going," she asked, "if I don't have the right outfit?"

We were able to enter the competition just in time, and she won two first-place ribbons: one for most photogenic, and the other for best smile. She was also one of three girls to receive a tiara. I don't think it was because of her outfit.

Once the beauty pageant was over and she had her ribbons and tiara, one of the judges introduced himself as a talent agent. He told me he'd be interested in working with her. I was shocked and excited. I started wondering if he'd seen the same thing I'd been seeing. I've always thought my little girl was special, and she's always acted like a star. He eventually got her involved with modeling and runway training at Page Park in Houston. She started doing a lot of print work, mostly advertisements for phone companies, toy companies, kids' clothing, and sports. She got a lot of work. I was tripping out.

Later that year, she was online and found a photographer in Austin, Texas, who was looking for an Asian girl. She told me about it, and I contacted him. He came to Houston and did a full photo shoot with her including location changes and lots of wardrobe changes. He turned out to be a world-famous photographer and has photographed her many times since then. He's even used me and her grandparents in some projects. Then she signed with a print agent in Austin, Texas. Now she had one agent in Houston and one in Austin. This was all very surreal for me; it all happened so fast.

In the meantime, a local Chinese radio station, privately owned and operated, was looking for people with radio experience who would be willing to donate their time. One of my friends knew I'd taken a course in broadcasting when I was in school. She mentioned me to the owner, and he contacted me. Since I had a lot of free time, I decided to do it.

Ironically, the show I was doing talked about Chinese marrying Americans and bringing their families over. It discussed how to raise kids with all the cultural differences. I enjoyed doing it a lot. It became very popular, with a lot of people calling in with questions and comments. I learned a lot doing that program. There are as many different views of the world as there are people.

Right before Yvonne's sixth-grade school year ended, she found out about a talent show in Orlando, Florida, being held by Fashion Rock. She submitted the form with her photo and got a positive reply. She was so excited when she showed it to me. I had no idea she had even sent it in. She had become more than a handful.

She was nine years old, and all of her clothes had to be bought at the top department stores. No Kmart, no Walmart. Now she told me I couldn't even buy anything for her to wear unless she was with me. I used to buy clothes and shoes on sale. Now she never wanted any of the stuff on sale. She was like a little diva; it was funny, really. Her big thing was posing. She was always showing me her latest fashion pose.

I wasn't planning to go to Florida or even leave Texas for her summer vacation that year. It cost a lot of money to go to Florida and enter your child in a competition. They don't pay any money unless you win first place, and this one had an entry fee. But she'd just completed the sixth grade with a perfect A+ year and would be starting middle school in the fall. Plus, she was so into her runway modeling. I decided for summer vacation that we'd go to Florida for the talent show.

She loved modeling and fashion and had been winning every little competition that was held around Houston. This would be a nationwide talent show. I figured we should go somewhere for summer vacation, so why not go somewhere different and let her try out what she'd learned at Page Park? We'd never been to Florida. She got so excited; all she talked about was Disney World.

In May of that year, just before she turned ten, we flew to Orlando and entered her in the competition. We arrived two days before the talent show, which was held three days in a row. Then we traveled around Florida and saw Disney World, of course. She didn't win anything at the competition, but I think it was a great experience for her, and we had a great time. It was a real eye-opener for her and for me. There was some great talent in that show.

She missed the stage call for her age group. She was in the restroom doing her makeup. I was yelling, "Come on, Yvonne! I see all the other kids going down the runway!" By the time she came out of the restroom, the teens and twenties were on the runway. She just jumped up there and did her walk along with the rest of them. Then the girl in front of her slipped and fell. I wasn't sure what Yvonne was going to do. People started to laugh, but she just went right on with her modeling. The crowd started to applaud her. I was so proud.

When she started seventh grade, she tried out for cheerleading and made the squad. Now she was always working on her cheers around the house and in the yard. It was all cheers, all the time.

Then I got a call from her school one morning, saying I had to pick her up. When I asked why, they said she was breaking school regulations. When I got there, I saw what the problem was. She was wearing a skirt that was entirely too short, and a too-small tank top. I don't know what her problem was. The girls had been told on the first day of school that they couldn't wear skirts that were too short or tank tops that were too small. They even had a high school girl and boy stand up on the stage showing how not to dress. I was mad as hell. I had to take her home so she could change clothes. She was marked down as late when I took her back to school. She usually rode the bus. That day, she did everything the school had said not to do.

Then, one day, she walked up to me and said, "Mom, we have to go to Hollywood."

"What are you talking about?" I said. "We're not going to Hollywood."

But we did go to Hollywood. She'd set up her own audition for a TV show.

I called the casting director to tell her we were not in Hollywood but in Sugar Land, Texas. I asked her if this was a paying job. She said first Yvonne would have to go through the audition process. She told me that my daughter was exactly what they were looking for. Once again, it wasn't an easy decision, but I didn't want to hold her back; I didn't want to let her down. I didn't want her to be limited like I was at that age, so I took her to Hollywood.

When we flew into Los Angeles, we checked into a hotel near the airport. The next day, I called a taxi to drive us to the audition in Santa Monica. So many Asian girls were there; I was shocked, since there aren't that many Asians in Texas. I thought to myself, *We probably made this trip for nothing. At least she can say she's been to Hollywood, though.*

She went through the audition process, and we decided to take a look around Hollywood. We took a cab to Hollywood Boulevard. We'd been there for only about two hours when my phone rang. She got the part! It was for *Globie's World*. What can I say? She is so good at whatever she does.

Once we knew she had the part, I contacted her father and told him we were in the Los Angeles area. Lu was still living in Los Angles at the time. He came and took us out to dinner. It had been four years since he'd come to Houston to see her.

I asked him whether he'd recognize Yvonne if he saw her walking down the street. "No; she's grown so much since the last time I saw her," he said. That made me feel like crying, but I held back my tears.

I told him how well my parents were doing with their dance studio in Houston and asked him how his parents were doing in China. He told me his parents were doing well, and his business was doing very well. I gave him pictures of Yvonne and told him to make copies to send to his family in China. We talked for a long time over dinner.

The next day, he took us to San Diego, and we went to Sea World. I've never seen Yvonne so happy. She had so much fun with her father that day. She took a lot of pictures with her father or with me, but finally she held both of our hands at the same time and said, "I want a picture with my mama and baba together."

We had the pictures made and then looked at the different options for mounting them. Her father asked her which ones she wanted. She wanted only regular pictures for the ones of just me and her, or him and her. When it came to the picture of all of us, however, she picked out a snow globe to have it mounted in. She still has it.

She slept with it every night for a while, but then I didn't see it for a long time. One day, I noticed it under the sink in her bathroom. She'd painted and scratched it. She'd thrown it in there like she was punishing it. Every time she sees her father, she's a mess for a couple of weeks. Then she finally calms down and goes back to normal. She's a very emotional person, and I know she loves her father very much.

After we left Sea World, Lu took us to dinner at a very nice Chinese restaurant right beside the ocean. It was a beautiful night, and we watched the moon as it bounced on the water. I felt so many memories coming back, along with emotions. I held back my tears this time. It was really hard, but I did everything I could to keep him from seeing any weakness. We talked for a while after dinner. He wanted to know all about Yvonne. He asked her a lot of questions about her school and her friends. He started telling us more about his business. Finally, Yvonne excused herself and went to the restroom.

As soon as she was gone, Lu asked me, "How is your personal life?"

I'll never forget the way he looked at me when he asked this. The tone in his voice, the look on his face—I'll never forget it. It caught me off guard. I wasn't ready for anything like that. I knew he'd been looking at me all day, but I didn't think he was still attracted to me. Now that I knew, I excused myself as soon as Yvonne returned from the restroom.

When I got into the restroom, I tried to pull myself together, but I started to cry. I knew I still loved him, but it wasn't the same. I loved him like a family member, not a husband. I loved him like the father of my child, but not like a lover. It made me feel terrible. What had happened to all the feelings I used to have for this man?

When we drove back to Los Angeles, Yvonne fell asleep in the back seat. We'd been quiet for a while, just listening to music. Then Lu turned the radio down and said, "I don't want to be single anymore, and I've met someone."

"How long have you known her?" I asked.

"About a month."

I didn't say anything. I just waited for him.

There was a long silence. Finally, he said, "I need my green card. My father had a heart attack, and I need to go to China right away."

"You mean, you're going to marry her?" I said. "Is that what you're telling me? And you've only known her for a month?"

"I have no choice. I need my green card," he said.

Again, there was a long silence. I had the most uncomfortable feeling in my stomach the rest of the way home. The only other thing he said to me was, "I have to go to my father."

"I hope your father is all right," I told him.

He told Yvonne good-bye, gave her a hug, and was gone. I could hear my father's voice in my head, saying, *If both of you weren't married to your pride, you'd still be married to each other. You're just idiots.* My father was probably right.

When we found out that Yvonne had the part for *Globie's World*, we were informed that the filming wouldn't start until a month later. I was also told that she'd need a work permit, which was something we'd never dealt with in Texas. I was also told that if she was going to work in Hollywood, she'd have to set up a Coogan Trust Account. This is basically a bank account in the name of both the child and the parents; it's court-secured until the child reaches the age of eighteen. It prevents parents from spending their child's earnings. This used to happen quite often. All of this happened so fast; it was like a whirlwind.

I've heard all those stories about parents trying to live vicariously through their children. The sports dad who couldn't make it as an athlete, bound and determined that his son will. The once-beautiful mom who drags her daughter, kicking and screaming, to all the beauty pageants. It was never this way with Yvonne and me. At times I've encouraged her to keep going, but this entertainment thing has pretty much been her idea. I've seen her rush home from a friend's house so she can make it to an audition. She'll even ride the bus by herself, two or three hours each way, when I can't take her, and she never seems to complain about it. She's just a girl who is a natural talent with her own drive and ambition. I shouldn't say she never complains, though—she's a normal teenage girl most of the time.

This was her first time on film. Everything she'd done up to this point had been print work, runway modeling, or dancing on stage. She was so happy to have a chance to show off her talent. The whole time she was at the film shoot, her face was glowing.

"Mom, it's way more fun than runway modeling or print work. It's more work and totally different, but I can speak, sing, and dance right in front of the camera, and they go to different locations," she told me. "I feel more alive. It's not just photographs of me posing different ways, and there's more than one take, not like theater, and I can communicate my feelings."

I was so happy for her.

After she did *Globie's World*, things were different—she was a legitimate actress now. She didn't want me calling her baobao anymore; she wanted me to call her Yvonne. My little girl was growing up right before my eyes. But I still call her baobao.

I watched her: each time she did the part, she got better. She said she felt like she was finally in the right place, doing the right thing, and everything made sense to her. She thought it was great how the sun shone all the time in LA, making the day feel longer. She thought LA must be a happy city. Remember, she was raised in Houston, Texas, a city that gets rain six months out of the year.

If you've ever been to Los Angeles, you know it's a beautiful city. In one day, you can see the snow in the mountains and also the ocean; that afternoon, you can hike in the Angeles Crest Forest; in the evening, you can sit down at the sky bar on the forty-ninth floor of the Western Hotel for a nice dinner, taking in a 360-degree view of the nightlife. You can even see the Hollywood sign from there. It truly is a great city. I know, because I've done all of these things.

While we were in Hollywood, we were approached by a management company who wanted to represent Yvonne. We told them that we were from Texas, and they said to stay in touch. I was surprised again but thought, *She just has the look.*

When we went back home, she continued doing print work all over Texas, along with different dance and theater shows. She stayed in contact with the management company and let them know what she had going on.

When we got home, though, we found there was a big problem with the number of days she'd missed from school. I'd gotten notices in the mail that said if she missed more days, she'd fail the year. I went to her school the next day and talked to her counselor, her teacher, and her principal, but it didn't help. I didn't understand; she had great grades, all As, but they said it didn't matter. They told me that in America, they also count the number of days that a student attends school.

Now it was becoming serious. I had to make a decision. I knew she wanted to keep doing this acting thing, and I didn't have it in my heart to tell her no. We made sure she didn't miss another day of school, and she passed the seventh grade.

As soon as the school year ended, the management company contacted us and asked if we could come to Los Angeles for the summer vacation. I decided to take her to see what she could do. During those three months, she booked eight jobs, half of them through the management company and half of them on her own.

For the three months we were there, I rented a place in Temple City, near Chinatown. It was kind of expensive—way more expensive than Houston. Yvonne immediately signed herself up for dance classes at a Chinese dance school, where she first learned points for ballet. She did so well at that particular school that she ended up teaching there for the whole summer.

When it was time for eighth grade to start, once again, she was in Hollywood, filming. I decided we'd move to Los Angeles. This was not an easy decision. First of all, the financial burden alone was a lot to consider. I had to go back home and talk to the family. My parents strongly disagreed; Tony disagreed; my friends disagreed. One of my friends brought me a whole list of reasons why we shouldn't go, such as: it was too early for Yvonne, she was too young, Los Angeles is a dangerous city, and so on. But we moved anyway, just the two of us. She's my daughter; I don't care. You only live once. If she has a chance to be all she can be, then I'm willing to go every step of the way with her.

XVII: The Big Move

I talked to the management company again and asked the owner of the company where the best place to live would be—Los Angeles is huge. She told me either Burbank or Studio City would be the best, and closest to most of the studios. She said Burbank was preferable since NBC, Warner Brothers, Disney, and Universal are all there.

I started looking for a house in one of those cities, and, in the meantime, I started transferring all her school records from Texas to California. Everything was extremely expensive, and I was really putting a strain on my marriage. This was my little girl, though, and I didn't want her to be held back in any way, for any reason. I'm glad we moved to California, although it's been a lot of trouble.

While we were in California for that summer, we went to Santa Monica, Studio City, and Pasadena. We went all over Los Angeles for her different auditions. When we went to Burbank, though, I was convinced this was the right place, because Yvonne loved it. She especially liked the mall and the whole downtown area. "Mom, this looks like a really modern city. I wouldn't mind living here," she told me.

"Living here?" I said. "You mean, living here instead of Texas? Is that something you'd really want to do?"

"Yes!" she said. "Then I'd be closer to my dad, and closer to Hollywood."

I realized she was taking all of this seriously, so I told her, "Yvonne, I want you to understand how big a sacrifice the family would have to make for us to move to California. I want you to be sure this is what you really want to do."

"I'm going to be an actress, Mom. I've always known I was going to be an actress," she said. "I'm going to be rich and famous, and all you have to do is take care of the house and help me with my clothes on the set."

It was the first time I'd hinted that I would make the move to California. She'd hinted about it, but I'd just ignored her until that point. I kept stressing to her that if we did make the move, there would be no turning back. "Very talented people come from all over the world to Hollywood," I said. "It's not easy, Yvonne."

"You just give me a chance and watch me go," she said.

I was convinced.

We went to the information booth at Burbank's city hall so we could learn more about the city. We rode by the schools and the different neighborhoods and talked about it some more. Every day, if we weren't doing anything else, we'd go to Burbank. I was surprised to find that there are four or five public libraries in Burbank, and it's not even that big a city.

I was also happy to find out that Burbank is its own city. It's part of Los Angeles County but not part of the city of Los Angeles. It has its own police and fire departments. Thanks to the big studios, it also has the highest household income. The city has a lot of movie theaters and restaurants—in Sugar Land, we had only one movie theater. In Burbank, I've never had to worry about her riding her bike, walking to school, or going to the park; it's a very safe city. It has crime, just like everywhere else, but it's no different from living in Texas. Yvonne likes how you can see the mountains from Burbank. Texas is so flat. I remember when we first got to California, she was so excited about the mountains.

I finally found a nice townhouse in Burbank, close to everything: grocery stores, movie theaters, coffee shops; even the mall she liked so much is within a few blocks of our house. This has been great for Yvonne. The school is within walking distance on one side of our house, and a park is right on the other side of the house. I decided to buy, because rent is so expensive. I thought if we did end up going back to Texas, at least the house would be an investment. If I rented, I'd just be throwing money away.

Getting Tony to agree with all this was not easy. He knows Yvonne is very talented. He basically had the same conversation with her that I did, asking her if she was sure this was what she really wanted. He told her she wouldn't have the same support as she did in Texas. It would just be Yvonne and me.

He had a different conversation with me. I know it wasn't easy for him to let us go. He loves us very much, but there was no way he could have moved with us; we're too established in Texas. Moving would have meant selling the store and our property. That would have meant completely starting over.

"I'll get you and Yvonne relocated to California, and I'll join you later," he told me.

"That will mean selling our business and everything," I said.

I told him I planned on getting my real-estate license in California so that I could shape my schedule around Yvonne's auditions.

"If she's successful," he said, "and if you can sell some property, then everything should work out. I'll be able to sell the business at that point."

That was our original plan. We made three trips back and forth from Houston to Los Angeles before we were completely moved. Two of those trips were nonstop drives, sixteen hundred miles each way. We stopped only for a fast bite to eat or to get gas. Yvonne slept in the car the whole way on both of those trips. But she had a real look of contentment and confidence during the days when we were moving. She had a new presence about her that I'd never seen before. My baby was coming into her own. This was going to be a whole new adventure and challenge for both of us.

Once we moved to California, she signed with the management company. Things didn't come easily, though. The first five months were full of auditions but no callbacks. During this time, Yvonne was so stressed; she missed her friends and family, was trying to adjust to a new school, and, on top of it all, wasn't getting any callbacks. She actually developed a rash on the side of her face and neck that lasted almost three weeks. The doctor said it was probably stress-related. When I talk to her about it now, she tells me that around that time she was going crazy. Then she says, "I don't want to talk about it, Mom."

I know my stress level was really high around that time. I thought Lu would be able to help us. I thought he'd visit Yvonne more often. I don't know what I was thinking. The first time she got sick, she asked me to call him. She told me she wanted to see her father. She was feeling terrible, so I made the call. He told me he was too busy. I knew he'd just gotten married, and they had a new baby. But Yvonne is his baby too.

The first two years we lived in Burbank, he saw Yvonne only every three months for only about four or five hours each time. He'd take her shopping and out to eat, and then he'd bring her back home. She was always happy to see him, but I could also tell she was disappointed that he didn't spend more time with her. Around this time, I found the photo of me, her, and her father underneath her bathroom sink.

Yvonne, being the way she is, didn't take things lying down. Instead, she decided to take up figure skating. In December of 2006, she won first place at the Pickwick ISI Winter Holiday Competition in Los Angeles. I didn't even know that she'd started ice skating at first. The last time I'd seen her on ice skates, she fell down right away and didn't want anything more to do with it. I knew she liked roller skating; in Houston, she'd go with her friends all the time. She was really good at it. Sometimes, she and I would go together. Now she'd gotten together with some friends from school in California, and they'd been going ice skating. The first time I heard about it was when she asked me for money to go to the ice rink with her friends.

"You don't ice skate," I said.

"I have been lately, and I like it. It's fun," she said.

I gave her the money, and she went off to the rink with her friends. The next time I knew she was going, I decided to drive her and her friends there so I could go in and watch her skate. As usual, I was amazed; she was really good. She'd met a girl at the rink who was taking classes. She told me she wanted to take classes too.

She was about to turn twelve years old, and for her birthday I got her a pair of skates so she wouldn't have to rent them anymore. I also got her a figure-skating outfit. Then we signed her up for the classes. You wouldn't believe it: in one month, she jumped three levels; in two months, she was at the top, starting to compete. It was because of her ballet and other dance training. It was mainly the ballet, though. She had perfect body form on the ice.

She'd also found a new dance school where she could continue her ballet lessons. The school, owned and operated by Russians, is one of the top ballet schools in the area. Through this school, she landed three different roles in a production of *The Nutcracker*. Of course, the problem was that rehearsals for *The Nutcracker* and rehearsals for the figure-skating competition were often scheduled on the same day, sometimes even at the same time. I started to worry that maybe she was taking on too much, but she insisted she was fine.

When it comes to competition, she's like a tiger with wings. She placed first at Pickwick ISI, and then she stopped skating as fast as she'd started. I can't keep up with her; I never know what she's thinking.

What can you do when your child is this driven? I guess the best thing to do is to try to go along with them. That's probably not the easiest thing to do, but it's what I have done with my daughter, and it seems to have worked so far. It's not easy watching your child grow up; they're never going to be exactly who you want them to be. I can't believe she's been working and earning money since she was five years old.

While all of this was going on in her life, I had managed to land a few parts for myself through her agent. Some print work, and several commercials. But my biggest challenge was studying for my real-estate license. I was having a hard time reading the legal stuff in English. She was twelve years old now and had her own activities. Then I noticed her hair started to look ridiculous. She's always cut her own hair; I've never taken her to a hair salon. Actually, I take that back: I did once. It cost me fifty dollars, and she didn't even like it. When we got home, she got the scissors out and cut it differently.

Now she had the sides long, but she'd cut layers up the back. She was starting to get work. She'd just done print work for Nationwide Insurance and JC Penney's back-to-school promotion. She was going for an audition for a Go Green commercial. It was the first time I really argued with her. She insisted on having her hair styled strangely. I finally let it go, and she did get the job.

I had the worst time when we moved to Los Angeles. Yvonne had so many auditions, but I couldn't find my way around the city. Everything was so new. Auditions are held all over the place; some were even in Orange County. I've gone as far as San Diego and San Francisco for auditions. Not just for Yvonne, either. I've worked for Wells Fargo and the shoot was in San Francisco, and that was where the original audition was held too. I had a map but had a hard time reading it. Every other day we were lost somewhere and always late.

I got a lot of parking tickets; they were so expensive. Money was really tight; money is still tight; I guess money is always a problem. But some way or another, we've always managed to overcome, and I'm glad I brought her here.

In 2007, she booked a commercial for the 2008 Olympics that were to be held in Beijing, China. The commercial was aired all over the world. This was a big ego boost for her. I think she really needed it at that time too. Things had been going so slowly. It was a rough time for both of us.

All the Chinese newspapers and magazines in the United States picked up the story about the Chinese American girl who was in the Olympics commercial. Several different articles were written, including interviews in the *Burbank Leader* and the Los Angeles *Times*. She was also given an incredible amount of exposure by the media in China. Including television, newspapers, and magazines. Every time anyone in China checked their e-mail on their computer they were seeing an article written about my little girl.

In the commercial, she said "I am not a failure; I am an athlete" in Chinese. And I was thinking to myself, *No, you're not a failure at all, baby.*

What an outstanding journey my life has been. I had a chance to train for the Olympics in Beijing, now my daughter was in a commercial for the first-ever Olympics to be held in Beijing. Who would have dreamed it?

One article in a Chinese newspaper talked about three generations of our family having close ties to the Olympics. Yvonne was the one who actually gave the family a face. How proud we are of her.

After six months of studying, I finally managed to get my real-estate license. I even sold a house in 2009 after having my license for two years and going through many, many listings. It was a three-and-a-half-million-dollar cash deal, the biggest deal to ever go through my office, and it was in the middle of the worst recession America had seen in a hundred years. For once, I was extremely proud of myself. I also felt very lucky. I made sure I spread the wealth around when I got that commission check.

Things had been bad before that, and they haven't been that much better since. It's bad for everyone; our economy is terrible right now. It's been really hard for Tony. The business at the store is much less than it used to be, and he hasn't been able to sell the store or the house.

On top of getting my real-estate license, I also started to get some acting parts myself. I started out just doing work as an extra since I was taking Yvonne all over Los Angeles. Plus, I needed money, even though being an extra doesn't pay that much. Every little bit helps. Even doing speaking parts on film doesn't pay that much, when you think about the time and expense involved. It's the residuals and the royalties that pay the big money. You don't get any of that money, though, unless you're in the union. So you're mainly paying money out of pocket on most of these projects. The idea is to build up a body of work so you have a good-looking resume. Plus, the more you work, the more popular you become. It's all a tremendous challenge.

The first thing I was offered was a commercial; then I got some print work. I did three more commercials, and finally I found myself on the hit TV show *24* during its seventh season. I've also done a lot of student films and music videos. Plus, I've done voiceovers for international airlines. If you're ever on an international flight and you hear someone over the intercom speaking to you in Chinese, it just might be me.

I was on the television show *1000 Ways to Die*, and I've done some theater with Yvonne. In 2007, Yvonne and I played mother and daughter in the movie *Still the Drums*. It was a huge thrill to actually be acting in a feature film with my daughter.

I haven't mentioned any of Yvonne's troubles yet. She was now thirteen years old, and they don't call them the "troubled teens" for nothing. She'd been going to public school, but as soon as her fellow students saw her in commercials and magazines and realized she was an actress, her trouble began.

First, rumors started to fly. Kids were calling her a whore and saying she was on drugs. Then Yvonne started to act out. She was caught shoplifting, skipping school, and charging girls money to have their hair cut in the school restroom. I have to say, I think that last one was pretty smart. When I was growing up in China, my mother would have been proud if I'd been making money like that.

At this point, Yvonne revamped her whole life. First she stopped figure skating; then she stopped taking dance classes. She changed the way she dressed and started dressing like a tomboy. She started riding a skateboard all the time. Then she got ticketed by the police for not wearing a helmet. That put an end to the skateboarding. I guess the helmet just didn't look cool.

She joined Tae Kwon Do and started singing and writing songs. She's very much into hip-hop and hopes to release her own CD in the future. Eventually she did start taking dance classes again, but she focused on hip-hop dancing this time.

These changes she made in her life seemed to help; change is always good. The changes were coming so fast, though, I couldn't keep up. I told her once, "Yvonne, when I was your age, just playing an instrument or doing any one of the things you've done would have been enough for me. Look at all the things you've done. Are you going to stick with any of them?"

"Mom, when you're a kid and you don't know what you want to do, you have to try different things," she said. "I'm trying to find myself."

"You're so good at everything you do, but as soon as you reach the top, you quit," I said.

"I get bored fast. Plus, I like a challenge," she told me.

What could I do with that? I had to just watch her go. But, I swear, some kids in America are very spoiled, including mine. She must think we're rich. I know that she knows we're not, but she acts like it sometimes. She has really expensive taste, and she always wants to take classes in something. But I like the fact that she always wants to learn something new. This is the reason I wanted to raise my child in America. She would never have had these kinds of opportunities in China.

Taking Tae Kwon Do classes helped her land a part in the stage production *Be Like Water*, which played in a downtown Los Angeles theater for one month. She doesn't particularly like theater; she says it's hard doing everything in one take. But she said she enjoyed this show because she had to learn how to use nunchucks, and she also got to learn some martial arts. Plus, she used some of her Tai Chi training.

The hip-hop dancing she'd been doing got her a part in the Wii video game *Ultimate Band*, where she was the "ultimate guitar girl." This was another big thing for her. When the video game was released, she was in all of the advertisements. One of her friends called from Texas to tell her she'd seen her in a magazine at the grocery store. That was how we found out. She also had a part in Disney's *Hannah Montana* around that time, and, later that year, she was featured in a beauty pageant on an episode of *iCarly*.

I couldn't believe it. What am I saying? I still can't believe it. I walked into the grocery store across the street from our house and picked up a magazine from the news rack, and there was my little girl. I bought ten copies; I couldn't help myself. I still have them. I don't know what I'm ever going to do with them, but I have them.

To tell you the truth, at this time you could also see my face at all the Wells Fargo ATMs around America. I'm always so caught up in what Yvonne has done that I forget about my own achievements.

Then her grandparents called, freaking out. I told them she'd done the Olympics commercial, but maybe they just didn't understand. When they actually saw her on their television, they couldn't believe it. They watch only the Chinese network, which was airing the commercial about ten times a day. My mother was overjoyed. She called me two days later to tell me that all she'd been doing was sitting in front of the TV, waiting for Yvonne's commercial to come on again.

I think she's been doing great; I don't think it's easy becoming a star. I hope, by writing this book, I can give some insight to parents of children who are striving for a career in acting or entertainment. I think it takes a long time unless you're really lucky. When you look back at their careers, you can see that most actors were in commercials and doing print work when they were children. I think it takes a certain type of child to do this type of thing. So far, Yvonne seems to be that type of child.

XVIII: Teenage Angst

One night, we were in Santa Monica, having dinner at a restaurant, when I got a callback for the Wii video game. This would be Yvonne's third trip. The call came straight from the casting director, who told me that the clients had been waiting for Yvonne for at least forty-five minutes. I told them she hadn't even received a call from her management saying they wanted to see her again. I told them we were in Santa Monica but would get there as soon as possible.

The audition was in Sherman Oaks, about thirty-five miles away. With no time to finish eating, I paid the bill and drove like crazy, fighting with all the heavy Los Angeles traffic. We arrived almost an hour later. They wanted her to wear the same clothes she'd worn the last time she was there, but I told them that would be impossible.

They must have really wanted Yvonne; the casting directors and all the producers, about seven or eight people, had waited for her for at least two hours. After all that, no wonder they hired her for the job. Of course, I got another parking ticket that day, but at least it wasn't a speeding ticket—or they all would have been waiting even longer.

The reason I just told you that story is that it's the kind of thing that happens all the time. Trying to be an actor is like always being on standby. You have to keep extra clothes in the car, plus makeup—you gotta have makeup. But it has to be the right makeup, packed the right way, so you can carry it with you. It's best to keep an extra pair of shoes in the car. There are all kinds of things you'd never think about until you're in that position.

You can't just leave town; you have to tell your team where you're going. Your manager, agent, publicist, if you have one—they all have to know when you'll be back. It's always hard for us to schedule vacations, especially around holidays. It always seems like one or both of us are busy.

The first year we lived in California, we went back to Houston for Yvonne's spring break, summer vacation, and Christmas. Now we're lucky if we go just for Christmas. Last Christmas, I had to leave Houston early so I could get back home to deal with urgent business. Yvonne stayed behind with her grandparents and flew home by herself a week later. Now Tony mostly comes to visit us, which isn't easy since he runs the store. When he comes to California, someone has to run it for him, which costs more money. God bless Tony; he's the main reason I've been able to bring Yvonne this far. There are no words to express how much I appreciate all he's done for us.

A lot happened for Yvonne at the age of thirteen. She started to find her own style; she changed her appearance; and she started making a lot of her own clothes. She pierced her nose and changed her hairstyle. All of this was upsetting to me, especially since she did the piercing herself—it could have been very dangerous. I told you, I'm never sure what she's thinking.

But she started getting work. I'd try to get her to dress more conservatively like the other girls when going to an audition, but when Yvonne dressed the way she wanted, she'd book the job. I'd make her take her nose ring out and dress a certain way, but later I found out she was hiding clothes in her bag, changing in the restroom, and putting her nose ring back in before she went in for the audition.

I'd always gone with her to auditions in the past, but suddenly she wanted to go alone. I wondered why, so one day I followed her. This is how I found out what she was doing. I was so pissed off. But what can I say? Whatever works, works.

I had so many problems with her around this time. I just couldn't understand. In China, when you're young, you always try hard to please your parents. You never talk back to them. She had the worst attitude. I couldn't believe how she'd talk to me sometimes. I really hated it.

"Mom, that's just the way kids are in America," she'd say.

"I know that's not true. Not all teenagers are rude to their parents and in trouble all the time," I'd tell her.

I will say, though, in China, a lot of your schooling concerns morals. A lot of the lessons are about how you treat others and who you yourself are as a person. I think something is missing in the American school system when it comes to those things.

In China, you're taught to respect your elders. When I was a little girl, if I saw an old man or a pregnant woman on the train, I knew they needed a seat, and I knew I was supposed to give them mine. I didn't think about it; it was just the right thing to do. Maybe I spent so much time making sure she could reach her dreams that I somehow let these things slip by. I know she's a good person, though. She just gets her head screwed on the wrong way sometimes.

Her management called with information about an audition for the *Dr. Phil* show. The episode would deal with troubled teens. I took her to the audition, and she got a callback with the good news. I really thought it was funny that she got the part, because at the time she was the ultimate troubled teen.

Her management called again, warning us about the sensitive nature of the questions that could be asked of Yvonne. Were we sure this was something we wanted to do? They said I should understand that I would be involved too. We talked about it and decided to go forward. I wanted her to do it because I thought she'd get a chance to see some kids who really were bad; maybe it would educate her a little. Yvonne wanted to do it because she's willing to do just about any part.

We went to the set. Other teens and parents were there, all different ages and races. They split us into two groups: parents in one room, kids in another. They made it so that the parents could see and hear the kids, but the kids could not see or hear us. The man asked them questions like what they thought about teens engaging in sex at an early age or having sex with no love involved. He asked us questions like how we dealt with our children when they got into trouble or how we made sure we raised them with morals so that they knew right from wrong.

Later, they took all the footage and edited it together, with Dr. Phil asking the questions. That's how they do it in show business.

All in all, I think it was very educational for us both.

Right after that, less than a month later, we both got booked again for a reality show whose name I forget, also dealing with troubled teens. During the filming, Yvonne revealed that people had taken her face from her MySpace page and used it on websites with adult content. She also said a lot of rumors were written about her on MySpace. I could tell these things had been bothering her. Yvonne also told the host that between this and the rumors about her at school, her teachers had become suspicious of her. She told him she used to like public school, but now she hated it.

When he asked me what I thought about all this, I told him, "This is the first time I'm hearing about some of it, but I've been having a lot of problems with her."

Then I realized, it's happening: all the bad things that go along with fame. The stories, the rumors, the lies. I thought to myself that this was probably just the beginning and that it was probably going to be hard for her. She's so sensitive and softhearted. She's going to have to learn to be private with her personal life and understand that she has a public image now. She's going to have to understand that some people just want to see you fail.

After the show, I got her to take down her MySpace page for a while. This made her very angry, but she agreed. I felt really bad for her, but if she was going to become a star, this was probably just the tip of the iceberg.

She told me that the most ironic thing was that a lot of the students who were talking badly about her would actually pay her up to one hundred dollars just to help them pick out their clothes and do their hair and makeup when they were going out. Jealousy is a terrible thing, and kids can be so brutal. Yvonne has never really had many friends since all of that happened.

She has had friends in the past who have stolen her clothes or got her into trouble some way or another, leaving her holding the bag. One time she was upset because one of her girlfriends had stolen the boyfriend of another friend. She told me she didn't want to hang out with that girl anymore. She knows the difference between good and bad. I'm glad she has good morals.

She and I both learned a lot from being on that reality show. I think it was a good experience for both of us, and it seemed to open up more dialogue between us. She'd been hiding a lot of her problems and feelings; she's still that way. But I could see that she started to mature and make better decisions for herself after we did the show.

She got a call about an audition that was asking for nonconservative, outgoing, teen-band-oriented people. She decided to dress totally weird. She wore high yellow boots and pulled her hair into ponytails sticking out in different directions. I argued with her about this, so she canceled the audition. However, she rescheduled it for later, when she knew I wouldn't be home. Her grandmother was staying with us at the time, because of all the trouble Yvonne had been in. Plus, I was working a lot and didn't have anyone to take her to auditions and be there with her while she was on film or photo shoots. I think my mom just wanted to get out of Texas for a little while.

Yvonne is a minor; it's not like I can just drop her off or let her take the bus. She has to have an adult with her all the time when she's on a set. So she dressed the way she wanted and had her grandmother take her.

She told me that when she walked into the audition, the producer said, "You've got it. That's exactly what we were looking for." This job was for *Camp Rock Guitar Star* for Disney Interactive.

"Okay; dress the way you want," I told her. "However you do your hair, your makeup, I don't care anymore. I think you know better than I do. I'm sorry."

Her very next audition was for Yum! Brands foods. Yvonne, feeling free, decided to dress weird again, and once again she got the job! She also booked a role in a feature film, in which she was an Asian gangster girl wearing her nose ring and all. They even put a big fake tattoo across her shoulder and down her arm.

Around this same time, she did a photo shoot for a poster for Pasadena Water and Power that made her look like a water thief. Her name on the poster was Tap-on-Tina. This poster ended up winning an ADDY Award in advertising. The poster was on all the bus stops across Pasadena for about six months. It was wild. Every time I was in Pasadena, I saw my daughter's face everywhere. After the posters, when she went to auditions, she was recognized more. Sometimes they even laughed and said, "You're Tap-on-Tina, aren't you?" Her friends and my friends kept calling to say they'd seen Yvonne's picture in Pasadena. I just thought, *Wow—we've come a long way.*

One day, she and I went to Pasadena so I could take a picture of her standing by her poster. Before I could get the shot, someone recognized her and jumped in with her. Then it was another person, then more people. It took me fifteen or twenty minutes to get a picture of just her.

I was as proud of her as I was when I gave birth to her. All the trouble, all the pain, all the money—I forgot about all of it when I saw the look on her face while she was signing autographs and talking to all those people. Right then, I knew for sure she was a star. She handled herself so well that day with all those people around her. She didn't get excited or nervous; she acted like it was just another day at the office. I wanted to be surprised, but at that point, I was just amused. She continuously makes me believe in her. Not just her talent, but her beauty as a human being.

I want to say to all those parents out there, be careful with your children. When they're playing a part, they can be influenced and become confused. Right after Yvonne was featured on this poster as a thief, she was caught shoplifting.

I asked her, "What the hell were you thinking? If you need something, I can buy it for you." I knew she had money with her.

"I just wanted to see what it would be like," she said.

Similarly, not long after she played the Asian gangster girl, she got a real tattoo on her left arm that says "Just Breathe."

Yet another example is that although she'd always drunk soy milk, she started to drink regular milk out of the blue one day and then suddenly booked a milk commercial. Is this life imitating art, or art imitating life? I'm not sure.

I don't want to talk too much about Yvonne's troubled teenage years. We all have our problems, especially around that age. I wanted to mention hers only to point out that despite her troubles, she's stayed focused on her goals. She's never stopped going to auditions and has continued to strive for more in life.

This is impressive when you think about the number of kids who drop out of school and all the teen mothers, all the hard drug users, and the ones who run away. Yeah! Yvonne hasn't done too badly, then. She's dealt with a divorce, a new country, a new language, a whole different culture. I've remarried, so she's dealt with a stepfather, and she's changed schools five times. Through all of this, she has slowly started to become someone very special. If it hadn't been for her pushing, I would never have done all the acting and entertaining I've done. I think she's just great as a daughter, as a person, and as a friend.

XIX: Home Schooling

The school Yvonne had attended in Houston required a school uniform. She never really liked the uniform, but she finally got used to it.

My daughter has always been a little different. Even in elementary school, she would take street clothes in her school bag, and as soon as the bell rang at the end of the day, she would change in the girls' room so that she could be the only one without a uniform. She knew she couldn't get in trouble because it was the end of the school day. I said something to her about it several times, but it never seemed to do any good.

Her new school in California did not require a uniform. On her first day, Yvonne was so excited that it took her forever to pick out her clothes and do her hair. She had on a necklace, bracelets, everything. "Do you think everyone will like me like they did in Houston?" she asked nervously.

"Everyone always likes you, Yvonne," I told her.

In seventh grade, she became the first-place high jumper in all of Burbank for girls in her age group. She competed with the Mustangs, her school's track-and-field team. She was also one of the principals in a dancing-and-singing group called Guys and Dolls, which won several first-place prizes, including a dance competition sponsored by Disney. Of course, she was still going to auditions and taking on any parts that came along. She always seems to find herself the center of attention.

This is when her dancing started to really excel. She'd been studying several styles of dance, spending a lot of hours at different studios. I can't tell you the amount of money I've spent over the years on her dance training. Now she was doing a lot of hip-hop dancing. I love to watch her dance; it's when she seems happiest. I've been watching her dance since she could walk. But now she's really become a fine dancer, with all the right moves.

It was around this time that she first mentioned home schooling. I thought she was crazy. She'd just started a new school, in a new city, in a whole new state. Sixteen hundred miles away from everything she knew, and she wanted to make another huge change.

When she was in eighth grade, I received a letter from the school saying that Yvonne was falling behind in her schoolwork and wasn't turning in her homework. This was not the first time a letter had been sent home. The others had been sent with Yvonne to be signed by me and brought back. Yvonne had been signing my name herself and returning them to her teacher. This letter came in the mail.

She'd also missed several days I hadn't known about. This was the first real fight I ever had with my daughter. Screaming, yelling, crying, saying things we didn't really mean, the whole thing. We'd argued about things in the past but never screamed and yelled at each other that way.

"Where did you go the days you missed school?" I asked her.

"I took the bus to Chinatown," she said, "or just hung out at the park all day."

I was mad as hell. It seemed like every day the phone rang at 2:30 p.m.; my heart would start racing and my body would shake, because I knew it would be either one of her teachers or the principal calling.

Soon Yvonne's school counselor called and told me that her grades had dropped too low and she'd missed too many days of school. Only four weeks were left in the school year. If she didn't do something about it, she'd fail eighth grade. Yvonne had to start going to school early to catch up on her schoolwork, and she had to stay late to work with a tutor after school.

Despite all this, she did complete eighth grade. Everyone came from Houston to celebrate with her; they'd thought she was going to fail. Then I started to think about the amount of pressure that had been put on her to succeed.

As soon as her graduation ceremony was over, Tony and I decided we'd take her and my parents to San Francisco, where Tony has family. I thought it would be good to just get her out of Los Angeles for a little while. We took the Pacific Coast Highway all the way from Los Angeles to San Francisco. Yvonne spent the whole trip staring at the ocean and pointing things out to us. When we got there, my parents really enjoyed Chinatown. We all had great fun on that trip.

"This must be what China is really like!" Yvonne said excitedly as we walked down the streets of Chinatown.

"Yeah, baby, a little bit," I told her with a laugh.

The next day, we visited Tony's sister in San Jose, right outside San Francisco. Tony has three sisters, one living in Germany, one living in Canada, and one living in America. I've spoken with the other two sisters on the phone, but the only sister I've ever met is the one living in San Jose. We've gone to visit her several times, and she's come to Houston several times. All her children are grown, with children of their own. Three of her grandchildren are around Yvonne's age, and she always has fun playing with them. All the adults hang around and chit chat, the kids play, and it's a fun time for everyone.

Once we were back home and the time came for her to register for high school, she started talking about home schooling again. I was infuriated. This whole move had been about her. The family had made so many sacrifices to get her this far. Tony and her grandparents were back in Houston. I had a long talk with her—well, it was really an argument. She was winning.

"I'm going to call Tony and your grandmother," I told her. "I want to see what they think about it."

"There's too much of a gap between us for them to know what I should do," she said.

I made the call anyway. Tony suggested it might be time to bring her back to Houston. That wasn't the answer I was looking for. My mother said the same thing, telling me I couldn't handle her by myself. Then she wanted to talk to Yvonne, so I put her on the phone. They talked for a few minutes. When I asked Yvonne later what her grandmother had told her, she just kept saying, "Nothing." She knows exactly how to push my buttons.

I wondered why she was so interested in home schooling. When I tried to register her for high school, the school mentioned how many days she'd missed during middle school for film shoots, as well as the days she'd skipped. They said she wouldn't be allowed to miss that many days of high school. The school did recognize the type of work Yvonne was doing, but they would make no exceptions.

Home schooling was something she and I talked about for a while. I didn't want her to miss out on having a prom, going to graduation, all the normal things that come along with public school. Things like meeting new friends and the activities she'd participated in through her schools in the past. I haven't written down every conversation we had about this subject. There were just too many.

"If you leave me in public school, I'll be in more trouble and probably fail. It will ruin my life!" she told me one night as she marched into her room, slamming the door behind her.

I thought more about it. I thought about all the extra activities she had outside of school, such as dancing and Tae Kwon Do. I thought about how I had to pick her up right after school so many times so she could run home to change clothes and do her makeup for an audition, and how she'd fall asleep in the car. Considering all this, as well as the things she'd revealed on that reality show, I decided it would be best for Yvonne if she was home schooled.

Finally, one night, I called her downstairs and said, "Yvonne, sit down. I need to talk to you."

"What is it now, Mom?" she snapped in that tone I hate so much.

"I'm not mad at you," I told her. "Your mother is Chinese; my English is not good; I went to school in China. I'm not going to be able to help you with all your schoolwork like your teachers in public school."

"You mean you're going to let me home school?" she said with the biggest smile on her face.

"High school is even harder than junior high," I told her. "You'll be on your own, and you'll have to organize your own time."

"Don't worry, Mom. I promise I won't disappoint you," she said.

Instead of registering her for public school, I registered her for home schooling. The whole time, she kept going to auditions.

Her eighth-grade year was her worst year—and it was the last year she attended public school. Her grades were terrible. Since she started home schooling, she has maintained an A average. I'm really proud of her.

I didn't know this at the beginning, but when students are home schooled, they must maintain a certain grade average or they won't be able to continue home schooling. Yvonne has managed to do this, and if she continues, she'll graduate one year early. It's very exciting to think of my daughter achieving such a goal.

With Yvonne home schooling, she had way too much time on her hands. She had to go to school only twice a week, Monday and Wednesday from 11:00 a.m. to 1:00 p.m., to turn in her units and take tests. The rest of the time was hers, except when she was auditioning or working on a photo or film shoot.

But there were hardly any photo or film shoots at that time. Hollywood was in the middle of a writers' strike, and not long after the writers' strike, the actors went on strike. This was right before the economy started to turn bad. It was slow, and sometimes I wonder what she could have done if the economy had been strong and Hollywood had been busy like it usually is. She'd probably already be huge. She's continued to work the whole time we've lived here, and she keeps getting bigger parts.

With all of her extra time, she decided to get a digital camera and started doing her own personal photo shoots. I think a lot of her photos are as good as some of the professionally done ones, even though some of them may be a little too sexy for her age. Sometimes I think she's growing up too fast.

In the middle of all this, she decided to start taking classes to learn to speak proper Chinese. Luckily she had a lot of free time, because this required her to ride the bus three hours each way, once a week. She speaks Chinese pretty well now, but her vocabulary is limited. She knows just the common words and phrases.

I think the whole home schooling thing is a good example of her knowing what she needs in her life and going for it.

XX: The Worst Fight Ever

She soon booked Bambi's Singing and Dancing Girls' Group in 2007, and we had to go to Hawaii so she could go on tour, singing the official song for the Honolulu Marathon.

First, I have to tell you the story of how she got this role. The group consisted of four girls who had been together for a couple of years. This year, one of them dropped out to go to college. They held auditions in Hollywood, where several thousand girls showed up for the part. They were looking for a girl who could sing and dance and was at least sixteen years old.

Yvonne had no problem singing and dancing, but she was only thirteen years old. Nevertheless, after several callbacks, it came down to two girls, Yvonne and another girl. The judges couldn't decide, so they left the decision up to the group's dance coach. After watching Yvonne and the other girl go through two or three rehearsals, he chose Yvonne. Later, he told me he'd chosen her because he really liked her attitude and her style of dancing.

The day we arrived in Hawaii for the marathon, a hurricane also arrived. There was a lot of talk on the radio and TV about whether there would even be a marathon. The weather was so bad that when we landed at the airport, I thought it was crazy! But it was also very beautiful. The airport in Honolulu is right by the ocean. Enormous waves were kicking up. I'd never seen anything like it.

Luckily, by the day of the marathon, it had cleared up. It was pretty bad, though. Trees had been knocked down, and some areas of Honolulu were without power. There was a lot of flooding. I knew it was the worst storm Yvonne had ever seen. The hurricanes we've been through in Houston weren't nearly as bad as this one. Of course, Hawaii is just a string of islands out in the Pacific Ocean.

Some thunder and lightning remained, and it rained when Yvonne and her new group did rehearsals that morning. However, they were on a stage with a roof. They also had light showers when they performed, but they still had a huge crowd. I could tell at the rehearsal that it was going to be a great show.

Yvonne loved the fact that there was a large Asian community there, and she had a blast. Come to think of it, I had a blast too. It was a great experience for both of us. We were in Hawaii, after all. It's so beautiful there.

I did worry about her, though. She was running with girls who were a lot older than she was; maybe this is where she started to pick up some of her bad habits, or maybe this just comes with growing up. When I was younger, I always liked learning things from the older girls. I remember my parents hadn't liked it, either.

The group actually performed five or six times while they were in Hawaii. They recorded a ten-song CD and did CD signings. They were also guests on *Hawaii on the Go*, the most popular radio and TV show in Hawaii, where they answered callers' questions. This lasted two weeks, and then we were back in LA.

In 2008, she was booked by Sports Entertainment of Los Angeles for the Los Angeles Marathon to be an Allegro dancer and singer.

This event was one big fiasco.

"Come on, we've got to go!" she yelled at me.

"We're going to be late!" I yelled at her.

But neither of us were ready. When we finally did get on the road, traffic was bad. The producer was calling, asking, "Where are you?"

"We're running a little late, but we're almost there," I told him.

The stage was on Sunset Boulevard, right where the runners were to start the marathon. When we got there, we saw that they'd blocked off several streets leading into that section of Sunset. We were late, and I couldn't get Yvonne to the stage. I parked my car, and as soon as we stepped out, a policeman told me, "You're going to get a ticket."

"I don't care. We've got to get to the stage!" I said.

He probably thought I was nuts, and I did get a ticket. I think it was like eighty dollars—damn it!

She was supposed to have a final rehearsal and a photo shoot and then hair and makeup before going on stage. She missed the rehearsal, and she missed the photo shoot. She went straight to hair and makeup and then straight to the stage. But she put on a great performance. It turned out to be a really good day.

She had some good experiences really quickly within just a few months. I could tell she was on fire then. When I saw her dancing on stage with all those other girls, I'd always think, *Damn, she's hot!* I know I'm her mother, but she is a great dancer and singer. She's just a great performer all the way around.

While we were in Hawaii, we were contacted by an independent producer who asked Yvonne if she was Chinese and how she got the spot in the commercial for the 2008 Olympics. He knew she'd been picked out of thousands of Chinese who have lived in China all their lives and speak perfect Chinese. He also knew about the tests each athlete in the commercial had to go through. Each one of them was asked which sport they were into. Yvonne said high jumping, so she had to do this, as well as jump hurdles. Each person was asked to do a bit in front of the camera, speaking their native language.

The producer told her he wanted to interview her for a documentary. She agreed; at the time, she thought she'd be playing a part in a documentary. It turns out that the documentary was about Yvonne. It was twenty-five minutes long and has aired many times in China since then.

The producer and his film crew followed her around, interviewing her and shooting film footage of her in school, at her Tai Kwan Do classes, at her dance school, and at figure skating. They filmed her going about her daily routine. I was so worried that this kind of activity was going to blow her head up out of all proportion.

She seemed to take it all in stride, though. She's never really had that big of an ego. All in all, they spent about three weeks filming just to get twenty-five minutes of footage for the documentary. It turned out to be another really good thing for her. They even did some shooting the day she performed at the Los Angeles Marathon. Between the documentary and the commercial for the Olympics, she'd opened another door for herself in China.

During the Christmas season of 2007, we went back to Houston. While we were there, Yvonne was invited to the Chinese Embassy, where they held a ceremony recognizing her for bridging the gap between China and America for the first-ever Olympics to be held in Beijing.

I was so proud of her once again. *Proud* is not even the word for it. I felt like I was in the clouds. I found myself on another emotional rollercoaster ride, but this time in a good way. Imagine if the president of the United States invited your child to the White House. How would you feel? That's how big a deal it was for me. I couldn't believe all she'd accomplished; I still can't. It was the biggest thing that had ever happened in my parents' lives.

"Our granddaughter got us formally invited to the embassy by the Chinese government," my father said. "Can you believe it, Yanyan? She's your daughter. The family loves her so much." The way he was looking at her, she might as well have been a gold medalist at the Olympics.

"I didn't make it to Beijing when I was her age, Baba," I told him. "But I gave you a granddaughter who's going to do so much more." He hugged me, and we both cried tears of happiness.

She also was awarded a plaque for being a goodwill ambassador by the Chinese Company World Famous Fame.

She was also given an award by the Chinese American media and a 2008 New Year's celebration party. My daughter was a star. She'd made it to the top in my eyes. She was only thirteen, but we were living in America, and even the Chinese government was acknowledging her achievements.

This Christmas and New Year's truly did make Yvonne feel like a star. Lots of parties and dinners revolved around her. All the family and friends were there for her.

In April of 2008, we got the biggest news of our lives. Tony called to say that we would both have to come back to Houston. He'd gotten a notice saying that my little girl and I had been granted citizenship. He gave me the date that we were to be sworn in as citizens of the United States of America: April 30, 2008. It had been more than ten years since my attorney had first filed the proper paperwork. I had been married all that time and holding a green card along with Yvonne, but neither one of us were citizens.

It was hard, even for Yvonne, even though she was raised in America. When I told her about it, she was surprised. "What?" she said. "I thought we were American citizens."

"No," I told her. "We've only been in America on visas, because I married Tony."

"What will this change for me?" she asked

"You'll have the same rights that any American has," I told her.

"Wait a minute, Mom." She had a serious look on her face. "Maybe I don't want to give up being Chinese. I thought I was an American all this time."

"If we don't become American citizens," I told her, "then your grandparents have to go back to China."

"What do you mean?" There was panic in her voice. "Why would they have to go back to China?"

"Because they're not citizens, either," I told her. "They can't legally stay here until I become a citizen and file the proper paperwork for them."

"Then we have to do it," she told me.

It was an emotional day when we went for the ceremony to be sworn in. I heard her voice in my head saying, *Wait a minute, Mom. Maybe I don't want to give up being Chinese.*

"Why are you crying?" Yvonne asked me. "You're supposed to be happy. You're American now."

"You're right, baobao," I told her. "We're Chinese at heart, and it's not easy giving that up. Always remember that you're Chinese. Never forget your heritage."

We cried and hugged each other.

When we got back home to California, she knew she was an American now, and she decided she wanted to use some of her new rights. She decided to legally change her name to Kharma, because all her friends had been calling her Kharma for a long time. So we went about the process of legally changing her name to Kharma.

It's hard; I've been calling her Yvonne for so long. I've called her Kharma only a few times since she changed her name. I still call her Yvonne or baobao, which means baby in Chinese. I guess Yvonne has become her stage name now that Kharma is her legal name. But in my heart, she'll always be Yangyang, even though her real name is Chang Lu.

She's always been mature for her age. When she turned fourteen, she decided she could stay out as late as she wanted, until the police picked her up and ticketed her for being out so late at such a young age. It didn't matter that she told the police she'd just talked to me on the phone and that it was only 12:30 a.m. No matter; the authorities stepped in. There is a 10:00 p.m. curfew in Burbank if you're under eighteen. I didn't know this at the time. Even after getting in trouble, she snuck out in the middle of the night a few times. When I found out, I got more scared and worried than angry. Anything could have happened to her. My best friend and I both told her that she'd been so blessed. We told her there were little girls like her who disappeared all the time. I swear to God, she was giving me gray hair.

Finally, Yvonne got interested in boys and started dating; this was a disaster. Her grades went way down again, and I received several notices from the school stating that she was falling behind in her schoolwork. Even though she was home schooling, she still had to take tests in front of teachers and turn in a certain number of units each month.

She started talking about giving up acting altogether. At this point, I was confused. I didn't know where she was headed. I tried talking to her, but she just pulled away and went into her room. More and more distance seemed to be growing between us.

One night, around midnight, the police caught her making out with a guy in a parked car; as a result, she had to go to youth counseling once a week for a few months. After this, she stayed home for at least two months and slept most of the time, hardly talking to friends or anyone except me, and then only barely. She stopped going to all her activities.

I had to call Tony and tell him to come as soon as he could. I told him something was wrong with her and I didn't think I could handle her by myself. First, I was so worried about her because she was just staying in her room all day, every day. Now she had fallen back into her games again. She had a new girlfriend she was running with, and she was starting to come home later and later at night. He flew in the next day. I told her to come with me to the airport to pick him up; she'd always gone before. Now she was lying on her bed and didn't even look at me. "I'm too tired to go with you," she said. "I'll see him when you get back."

I was so disappointed in her. I knew she was tired; all she'd been doing was running here and there and everywhere with her new friend. Being disappointed in her is the worst feeling. I hate it. That's the only time she's ever missed picking up or dropping off her stepdad at the airport.

Tony stayed for a week and tried to talk some sense into her. She kept saying that there was too much of a generation gap and a cultural gap between us. What the hell does that mean? When you're in the wrong, you should just say you're in the wrong. When you find yourself in trouble, you should listen to the people who care about you. But Yvonne didn't seem to get any of these concepts. She can be so hardheaded sometimes. I have noticed something, though. When I say something to her and she acts like she's not listening, later on she'll actually do what I'd been telling her. So I hope some of it sinks in.

The youth counseling seemed to help, but there was still the issue of her acting. She'd started talking about being a psychologist. I've always wanted her to go to college, and I don't care what major she chooses, but I started to seriously wonder if she was giving up.

"You can go to college when you graduate from high school. I want you to," I told her. "But you'll never be this young and vibrant again."

"What does that have to do with college?" she asked.

"You have your whole life ahead of you—I hope that's going to be a lot of years—to do a lot of things," I said. "But if you quit now, you'll always wonder what could have been." I told her she'd always regret giving up later in life.

Tony asked me again if I thought it was time to take her back to Houston. This time, he really tried to convince me.

"No, she's not done yet," I told him. "I know she can do so much more."

"Maybe you should tell her you're taking her back to Houston," he suggested.

"I already threatened her with the idea," I told him. "She promised me she'll straighten up her act. She wants to stay in California."

I knew he was frustrated with the fact that he wasn't going to be able to change my mind. Of course, the business in Houston had been slow, and he often stressed to me that we needed to save money. We were making two house payments, and the store was our main income.

What made it all worse was that Yvonne had recently broken off with the boy she'd been seeing. He got angry about it and gave the password to her MySpace page out to different people. She made me drive to his house because she wanted to confront him. When we got there and he came to the door, she attacked him. I had to jump between them. I have to say, she was handling her business pretty well. At least I know she can take care of herself.

When Halloween came around that year, a friend and I dropped Yvonne off at a big Halloween party she'd been planning to go to for weeks. She disappeared for two days. She sent me a text message the day after the party saying she was fine, and then she turned her phone off. I was at my wits' end, ready to call the police, when she finally showed up at home.

She said her phone was out of power and she'd had no charger. I was so angry. *All her friends have cell phones; she could have used any one of them*, I thought to myself. I lost it. I yelled at her, telling her how I'd been online and on the phone with T-Mobile to find out who she'd been in contact with. I told her I'd called all her friends and their parents, trying to find her.

When she tried to make light of the situation, I shoved her out of the way and grabbed her laptop from her room. I ran downstairs; she followed close behind me.

"Give me my laptop! My father bought that for me!" she screamed.

"Who's always been here for you?" I asked. "Your mother! But this time you've pushed me too far. If you think I won't smash this computer, just try me!"

"No! You're going to give me my computer!" she screamed.

She was only fifteen years old. We were living in Los Angeles, California, one of the roughest cities in the world. And she thought she could just stay out all night without me knowing where she was? She thought it was all right to scare the hell out of me? I smashed the computer on the floor. She started crying, ran back to her room, and slammed the door. To this day, she still reminds me that I smashed her computer every time we argue about anything. I don't care. She's got to learn that you can't push Mom too far. I have my limits too.

I wrote down some rules on a piece of paper: no Internet access, ten o'clock curfew, no more smoking (I'd just found out she was smoking), keep her room clean, and stop cutting her own hair. "If you can sign and date this for me, we'll have no problems," I told her. "Otherwise, you might have to go live with your father."

I would never let her live anywhere else, but I wasn't going to let her know that. She didn't sign it right away. She got angry and ran to her room again. I didn't know what I was supposed to do.

I got on the phone with Lu and told him about all the trouble I'd been having with Yvonne. Until that point, he'd thought his daughter was a perfect little angel. I'd hidden everything from him, because I thought there was nothing he could do about it. We decided she should stay with him four days out of the week for a couple of months. The only thing that would change this was auditions. I didn't let her know that, though. I just let her think she was moving to her father's unless she signed my list of rules.

When her father picked her up, we stood there and talked about the situation for a few minutes. The last thing I did, after hugging her and telling her I loved her, was give the piece of paper to her father. "When she signs it, she can come back to my house," I told him. "Otherwise, I'll be sending the rest of her things."

I wanted her to believe the whole thing. To this day, she doesn't know that her father wanted to send her back to China right away. He wanted to do to her what they used to do: make her stay in a village somewhere so she would have no phone, no Internet, no contact with the outside world. She has no idea. It would have been like jail for her.

Yvonne didn't like staying with her father at first. In the past, they'd had only short visits, and she'd never spent the night at his house. Once she went, though, she told me it was good to spend time with him, and I know they became a lot closer. That had been my plan all along. Since moving to California, I'd had the hope that her father would spend more time with her. Lately, he has been. I think it would be a shame if he never knew her, and she never knew him.

This was the worst fight Yvonne and I had ever had. Things had been changing in our lives so quickly. The worst thing that could happen was losing my daughter, or her losing me. I don't care if she's a star, I don't care if she's gay, I don't care if she has piercings or tattoos, I don't care what she does—I love my daughter. But when she scares me like that, I can't help it. I lose control.

After she left to go stay with her father, I had another breakdown. Memories came flooding back. I gave Lu an ultimatum once, and it didn't go my way at all. What if I'd made the same mistake with Yvonne? What if she never came home? What if her father really sent her to China? I started thinking how hard it must be for Lu to accept this new truth about his beautiful young daughter. I knew he was having a difficult time with it all. He was remarried, with a new son of his own. I wasn't sure exactly how he was going to handle her. I knew I was taking a really big risk, but I felt like it was time to throw the hammer down. I was either going to lose her now, or she was going to change.

The next morning, I had a text message from her asking, "When can I come back home?"

I sent her a message right back, saying, "You're not coming back home until you sign that piece of paper for me and change your attitude. I love you. Call me if you need me."

I didn't hear back from her until later that night, when she called to tell me goodnight and that she loved me too.

She stayed with her father for five days. She can be a really stubborn girl. I know she was testing me, because I got several text messages from her during those five days. I know she was enjoying spending time with her father, but she doesn't like his wife very much. At any rate, she eventually signed the rules. It was the evening of the sixth day, around four o'clock. I got a text message from her, saying, "All right. I'll sign your piece of paper." She signed and dated it in front of her father and me when he dropped her off. I wouldn't say she's never broken any of those rules, like cutting her own hair or staying out too late, but she's a lot better now.

XXI: Trip to China

After a lot of grief between Yvonne and me, after several trips back to Houston to be near the family, after her grandmother came to stay in Los Angeles with us for a while, and after Tony made several trips from Texas to Los Angeles, things started to calm down. Yvonne had a new attitude and seemed to be staying out of trouble. It was nice to have my little girl back, but it didn't last long.

She had a boyfriend, a nice Thai boy, with no tattoos or weird piercings. He dressed normally and had nice hair; he was pretty clean cut. I sat him down and went over all the rules with him. No drugs, no alcohol, home by ten, no smoking, no shoplifting, if you get my little girl in any trouble, we're going to have a big problem. Yvonne started to stay home most of the time; the only problem was that he was always there.

In 2009, Hollywood dried up, the economy sucked, and I got more work than Yvonne did. Though both of us continued to go to auditions, all Yvonne got was a broken heart from a bad relationship. It was sad; it's always hard the first time your heart gets broken. She was my little girl just yesterday, and now she thought she was in love. I felt really bad for her. She'd let all her girlfriends go, because she'd spent all her time with him.

"That's why I didn't want you to have a boyfriend yet," I told her. "You're too young to handle it." Yeah, right—I'm sure that made her feel better.

In December of 2009, just when it seemed that the year had been a waste, she landed a nationwide milk commercial. Once again, it was a much-needed ego boost for her. Of course, she pulled it off easily!

Since she hadn't worked for the entire year, I hadn't realized that her work permit had expired. This was a big problem. When she got the callback for the milk commercial, she found out the filming was to start two days later. The day after the callback, I booked a part myself on the TV show *1000 Ways to Die*. That gave me only one day to get her work permit renewed.

First thing the next morning, I went to Yvonne's school to get their okay for her to have a work permit. Then I got my friend to take it to the child labor department for me, because I had to rush off for my own film shoot. I was late, but everything worked out.

Once the filming for *1000 Ways to Die* had wrapped up, I rushed home to get Yvonne to the fitting for the milk commercial. Again, we were late.

The next morning, we arrived at the studio for the actual film shoot. I was feeling ragged and worn down. Yvonne seemed to be full of energy, though. I've always thought we make a good team.

"Mom, what's wrong with you today?" she asked. "You look like you're still asleep."

"Mom isn't young like you are," I told her. "Where do you get all the energy?"

"If I could give you some of mine, I would," she said.

When I find myself feeling down and out, she's always there to pull me up. When she's down and out, I'm there for her to do the same. Luckily, both of us are never down and out at the same time. If we were, though, we'd be there for each other.

The commercial was called "Pass the Milk." It involved four families: Asian, Caucasian, African American, and Hispanic. In the commercial, each family passes the milk to the next family straight through the refrigerator. If you've ever seen this commercial, then you've seen Yvonne.

In December of 2009, we went home for the holidays. On the flight to Houston, Yvonne told me, "Mom, I think 2010 is going to be a great year for me."

It was after midnight on New Year's when I got a phone call from a reporter who had written several articles about Yvonne in the past that were published in a Chinese newspaper in Los Angeles. The reporter said she had a friend who'd read some of the articles and had seen the commercial Yvonne had done for the Olympics. The friend was very interested in meeting her.

When we returned to California, I set up a meeting with him. At the meeting, he told us that one of the biggest producers in China was in Hollywood and also wanted to meet Yvonne. At that meeting, we found out we'd be going to China, where she would film two episodes of the most popular TV series in China, *Journey to the West*. It deals with ancient tales of gods and heroes, dragon kings, underwater castles, Buddhist scriptures, self-discipline, and enlightenment.

This was amazing for my parents. To them their granddaughter had already made it, but now she was a mega-star in their minds. My mother is a huge fan of the producer/director of *Journey to the West*. She's seen everything he's done. When they heard that their granddaughter was going to be working with him, they lost it. All they kept saying was that she was going all the way to the top. My father mailed me the whole history of *Journey to the West*. *Journey to the West* started out as a book called *The Monkey King*, then a movie, and finally a television series. Yvonne acted like it was just another day.

Her big problem was that her role required her to learn to speak her lines in proper Chinese within two weeks. She didn't receive the script until one week before leaving for China, and filming started the day after arriving in China. This is another example of life imitating art. She'd chosen to take lessons in speaking Chinese just months earlier.

Weeks before this, she'd started getting phone calls and text messages from her ex-boyfriend. She told me he'd called and wanted to see her.

"What did you tell him?" I asked.

"I told him I'm really busy right now," she said. "I told him we're leaving for China soon."

"What did he say?" I asked.

"He thought we were moving back to China." She laughed.

I thought that was pretty funny myself. She was too busy. There was also an issue with her school. They said she had to turn in the entire month's work in one week, or she'd fail the year. Once again, somehow, she pulled it all together. When she's down for the count, she really kicks it into gear.

She kept asking me for advice about the boy and what to do. But I had my own problems and was caught up in all the things that went into getting ready for the trip to China. I didn't know what to tell her. "You should worry about yourself," I told her. "Keep your heart closed, and concentrate on school and your career. You're too young for a boyfriend."

"Mom, it's too late for that," she told me. "I need some real advice."

"That is real advice," I said. "Advice from a mother who loves you. I wouldn't steer you wrong."

I had finances to deal with; our passports and visas had to be renewed. I had all kinds of things on my mind, and she did too. He'd picked the worst time to start calling her again.

My friend and I kept asking her if she was excited about going to China. She would just say, "Yeah, but I'm a little nervous, and I have so many things to prepare for."

The day my friend dropped us off at the airport, however, Yvonne looked at us and said, "Now I'm excited."

Inside the airport, both of us started to giggle like little girls getting away with something bad. Yvonne and I were on our way to China. It had been twelve years since we'd been there; last time, she was not quite three. I knew she didn't remember anything about China. This was one of the greatest days of my life—returning to my country with my beautiful daughter, who was becoming a star. Now she was international; next the world.

We got on a plane at Los Angeles International Airport for a seventeen-hour flight. I'd been dealing with so many things to get ready for our trip that I'd forgotten about the package my father had sent me via e-mail. I'd only glanced at it quickly.

"Look at what your grandfather sent us," I said.

She looked at it and got a smile on her face. "Mom, I can barely read any of this. It's all in Chinese."

It was the whole history of *Journey to the West*. "How many of these words can you actually read?" I asked.

She got all excited. "Oh, I know this one, and this one, and this one," she said while turning the page. "And I know these two too."

In the end, I realized she knew only a few of the words. I started translating for her. We had fun with that until we both finally fell asleep.

Eventually we landed in Seoul, Korea, for a six-hour layover. The first thing she saw was snow, something she'd never seen except in pictures or on television. All she wanted to do was get to the snow, but we weren't allowed to go outside the airport. This was pure torture for her. I tried to get her focused on other things. We started going over her lines; I wanted to make sure she was saying them in proper Chinese. Every time I had the chance, I made her go over her lines. I started explaining more about *Journey to the West* so she'd understand more of the tradition behind it.

Finally, we were on the plane again; and four hours later, we landed in Beijing. Now she could get to the snow. Not only was there snow on the ground, but is was also coming down hard. China was experiencing its worst winter in sixty years. Whole areas of China were completely snowed in that year. The weather got so bad, even cargo planes were grounded, so those people had no relief. So basically Yvonne went from sunny California straight into the worse blizzard ever. You should have seen the look on her face when we landed at the airport.

She was so excited to be standing there with snow falling all over her. "I can feel it melting on my face, and it's so cold," she kept saying.

She was trying to catch snowflakes in her hands. I loved watching her playing in the snow that day. She got her video camera out and had me take shots of her walking in places no one had yet stepped. We had a snowball fight, and I showed her how to build a snowman. It was great fun that day.

"Why is it so damn cold here?" she finally asked me.

"It's wintertime in China, baobao," I told her. "This is not sunny California." The wind blew so hard that she held on to me, and I grabbed a tree. We decided to find our hotel. The hotel room was cold even though it had a heater. The temperature outside was below freezing. Yvonne thought a hot shower would do the trick. But when she went into the bathroom, there was no shower—there was only a toilet and a sink. No tub, no nothing! She came into the other room and said, "Mom, where's the shower?"

I went into the bathroom and came out with a surprised look on my face. "I don't know. When I lived in China, we didn't have a shower," I told her, "but we did have a tub."

"I'm freezing, and there's not even a tub," she said.

I wanted to laugh at the tone in her voice, but I thought it best to keep it inside. Five minutes later, she was curled up in the bed, fast asleep.

I could see that there was some kind of contraption hanging from the ceiling in the bathroom, but I had no idea how it functioned. I felt bad for her. She couldn't understand why I didn't know what was going on. I told her later that everything in China had changed so much since I lived there.

The next morning, I got the hotel staff to show us how to operate the shower. It turns out you have to turn on an electric heater, which heats about five gallons of water in twenty to thirty minutes. Then, standing beside the toilet, getting toilet, sink, and everything else in the room wet, you can take your shower.

Yvonne thought it sounded plausible, so we turned the heater on. "You see that container hanging from the ceiling?" I said. "That's all the hot water you'll have."

The next thing you know, she was pissed off and screaming because the water was cold and she was covered in soap. We've all been there.

That morning, we had to take a shuttle to the CCTV Filming Foundation, where all filming takes place in China. It's basically a big complex like Universal Studios in Hollywood, but it's located in Zhuozhou City, in Hebei Province. It usually takes two and a half hours to get there from Beijing, but, because of the snow, it took almost four hours instead. Though the shuttle had heat, the temperature was so cold outside that it was still cold inside the shuttle. The ride was miserable, but the view was incredible.

"It's unbelievable," Yvonne said. "It's like a whole world of snow."

During the trip, she kept seeing different things from the window and asking about them. "Mom, what's that?" she'd ask. I'd try to explain, but before I could, she'd say, "Hey, Mom, what's that?"

She couldn't understand why all the small trees and shrubs were covered with plastic. I told her it was so cold that they'd freeze and die without protection.

"No way! Really?" she asked.

"It keeps the wind and snow off of them," I told her.

She thought it looked weird. I guess it did look weird, unless you knew what the wrapping was for.

"Why is everyone blowing their horn so much?" she asked.

"In China they do that as a common courtesy so you'll know they're coming," I explained. "It's not like in America, where they only use their horns when they're mad at someone." She thought that was pretty humorous.

We'd been given military coats when they picked us up at the Beijing airport. Yvonne didn't want to wear hers; she didn't think it looked good. She put it over her legs to keep warm instead. But when we arrived at the CCTV complex and she was facing six hours of wardrobe and makeup, she decided to wear the coat.

When we first arrived at the television studios, we were surprised to see all the movie sets still standing from movies like *Crouching Tiger, Hidden Dragon,* and the Jet Li films. It was pretty cool walking around inside those movie sets. I remembered taking her to Universal Studios in Hollywood when she was seven years old. Now she was fifteen, and I was taking her to China's equivalent of Universal Studios. I could see her excitement. Even though she'd been raised in America, I could see she was Chinese at heart. The closest she'd come to seeing that culture was Chinatown in San Francisco. When she saw the temples in China, she was blown away. She just stood there saying, "Wow!" I can't even explain her reaction.

The reason for the six hours of wardrobe and makeup was that the show she was acting in was based on the Tang Dynasty. Their hairstyles and clothing can be very complicated. It takes professionals a long time to assemble it all. She had five different people doing just her hair and outfit, plus a makeup guy. The hairstyles, clothing, and body language were something she'd never experienced before. She had more problems with her body language and mannerisms than she had speaking proper Chinese.

In old-world China, a female was not to look a male straight in the eye; she was supposed to be shy and reserved at all times. If she smiled, she was to do it with her mouth closed, with no teeth showing. All these things were a problem for Yvonne, because she'd been raised in America and had a very outgoing personality. Even though she can be shy at times, I wouldn't call her reserved.

Filming lasted almost one week, fifteen hours a day. In America, a child is allowed to work only six hours a day on a film shoot. In China, you're considered an adult at sixteen. She was fifteen and a half at the time—that was close enough. The wardrobe and makeup were so extensive that they added almost five hours to the shooting time, making it about a fifteen-hour day. Of course, she handled it well. After all, she's a professional.

I don't want to sound like I'm bragging about my daughter, but she really is a natural. She's never had any formal acting training. She just recently decided she might take an improv class. I'm always so impressed every time she does a part, and it's not just me. The people she works with always seem to be impressed too. That gives me validation. Otherwise I'd think I felt this way just because I'm her mother. So many times, someone has said to me, "It was a pleasure working with your daughter. She made everything so easy."

By the end of the first fifteen-hour day of filming and costumes, neither one of us had showered in three days. This is a girl who normally showers twice a day when she's at home. She told me she was frozen to the bone; she'd never been in such a cold place. She said all she wanted to do was get to our room and take a good hot shower.

We were staying at the studio's housing, provided for entertainers. When we got to our room, the first thing she did was check out the shower situation. She was so happy to find that there were a normal bathtub and shower.

"Mom, all I want is a hot shower," she told me.

She took off her clothes, turned on the water, and waited, and waited, and waited. There was no hot water. She stomped out of the bathroom, angry and confused. "You have to find out what the problem is right way!" she yelled.

"All right, all right, calm down. I'll see what the problem is," I told her.

I did find out what the problem was. Hot water was available for only two hours in the morning, from six to eight, and for two hours in the evening, from eight to ten. With her filming schedule, showering was almost impossible. She was so angry, I could see steam coming out of her ears. I couldn't help it; I had to laugh, which made her even angrier.

Yvonne was the only foreigner to ever play a role in *Journey to the West*. Everyone on the set knew this and knew she was from Hollywood. They all loved her, including her hairstyle and clothing. They had a lot of questions about living in America, which she was happy to answer. She told me it was always great to make new friends. When she talked with them, she used Chinese, English, and broken Chinese. Sometimes I translated for her. All of this improved her Chinese greatly.

She was featured in two episodes of *Journey to the West*, the first and second parts of a story in which a mother is trying to marry off her three daughters. She played the youngest daughter. The other two girls were twenty-one and twenty-six. They were supposed to be sixteen, eighteen, and twenty in the roles they played. Yvonne was the only one close to the right age.

I watched my daughter grow in leaps and bounds in one month. It was so funny to watch her try to walk and run in traditional Chinese shoes. It was incredible seeing her dressed that way, with her hair pulled up the way they used to wear it, wearing traditional Chinese clothing. I was in awe! Everyone kept telling me how beautiful she was.

It was so cold you could see their breath when they spoke on film. She was freezing her ass off and told me her head hurt badly from the ornaments pinned in her hair. But I know she had a great time there.

After the filming was complete, I took her and the two other girls to a restaurant for dinner. We had so much fun that we ended up back at our room, where the girls stayed up most of the night talking. They exchanged e-mail addresses and contact information the next morning. They took a lot of pictures together and were crying and hugging. It was very emotional for Yvonne.

The show's producer told us we could stay at the filming complex for as long as we were in China. I liked the idea because it would have been free, but I have friends in Beijing. I hadn't seen them in many years, and with the shower situation, I thought it was best if I could find a really nice hotel for Yvonne in Beijing.

She'd done such a great job, working such long hours for so many days in a row. I wanted to show her around Beijing. She'd been through a lot at this point, and I didn't want her to have a bad impression of China. I thought we would go live it up a little. All we'd seen at that point was the filming complex, and it was near a small town. I wanted to show her a big Chinese city.

When we got to Beijing, I asked her where she wanted to stay. "The Marriott or Hilton would be great," she said. We checked the Marriott, and I knew right away I wouldn't be able to afford one of the top hotels. Free trade truly has hit China. The Marriott in Beijing is more expensive than the Marriott in Los Angeles or New York. Even though this meant I couldn't afford it, I thought that was just fantastic.

I'd been worried since leaving America that Yvonne might get sick. She'd been going nonstop for days, taking on so many things in such a short time. But when we finally found the nice hotel we were looking for, I was the one who got sick. I couldn't get out of bed for an entire week. One of my friends came—an old classmate named Cuihong. She and Yvonne took care of me.

This trip to China brought the two of us closer together. When I was sick, Yvonne had to get food for me in a city she knew nothing about, with a language she barely speaks, but she handled it.

It seems like each time I've traveled to another country, I've gotten sick, especially when it's on the other side of the world. I've heard that this happens to a lot of people. I don't know what it is, but it sure happens to me. It leaves me flat on my back.

Let me tell you about the hair salon that was in the downstairs lobby of our Beijing hotel. Since I was sick in bed, Yvonne was very bored, so she decided to go to the salon and have her hair done. This was the first time she'd ever said she was going to a salon. She had her hair washed, dried, styled, colored, and curled, and she had extensions put in. She had to come back to the hotel room to get money from me to pay for it.

She had her own money, but it took all of hers plus some of mine. When Cuihong asked how much it was, she was shocked: it was 4,500 Chinese yuan, which would be $650. This was the first money Yvonne had ever spent to have her hair cut; she'd always cut it herself. I thought she deserved it—because to me she was becoming a little diva. I know how expensive that much work can be in America. It's not cheap, especially when they use real hair for your extensions.

Cuihong took her back to the salon, saying they were trying to cheat her. When they arrived at the salon, the man told my friend that Yvonne had wanted the best of everything: the best shampoo, the best conditioner, the best hair for her extensions, the best color to match. He felt so bad that he gave her back some of the money.

Yvonne was very angry. She hadn't wanted to go back and ask them for anything. "That was the top stylist in the salon, Mom," she told me. "Three different people spent almost six hours working on my hair." She went back the next morning and gave the man back the money. He still felt so bad that the rest of the time we stayed in that hotel, they washed, dried, and styled her hair every day for free.

The salon staff also took her out to bars and out to eat, and she went to shoot pool with them. She had a lot of fun with them. I have to say, her hair looked good. I'd never seen her with wavy, curly hair like that. When I started to feel better, I went and had them put extensions in my hair too. Yvonne helped talk me into it, but I wanted to go thank them anyway for taking such good care of my daughter.

Yvonne also went out a few times with Cuihong's son, Zhenli. He took her to Tiananmen Square, Old Beijing, and the Olympic stadium—all over the place. It must have been great for her to stand at the Olympic stadium after doing the commercial for the Olympics. She told me later that Zhenli called her Banana, and she didn't know why at first. Then she found out it was because she was Chinese but had been raised in America.

"He told me I'm yellow on the outside, but white on the inside," she said. She was so happy when she told me this. She thought it was a perfect metaphor.

She also told me later that she loved China and could see herself going back there many times in her life.

The year of 2009 was long for Yvonne. She went through a lot of changes very fast. She's so mature for her age, in so many ways, that it causes her a lot of problems. She was fifteen now, becoming a beautiful young woman in front of my eyes. I'd always thought she had a pretty face, now she started carrying herself like a lady, instead of a child.

I took her out to a restaurant one night so I could talk to her about writing this book. I wanted to know what she thought about the idea of me telling our life story. At first she thought it was strange, but the more we talked about it, the more she warmed up to the idea. When the waiter came to our table, I ordered a glass of wine, Yvonne said she'd have the same. The waiter asked for no ID from either of us, so I let it ride. The waiter brought us our wine, but then the manager came over and asked asked her for her ID. Well, obviously, Yvonne had to give back her wine, but she thought it was funny that I'd let her order it in the first place and that they brought it to her. Sometimes you can't tell how old or young she is.

She told me that when we were in Beijing, no one asked her for her ID when she went to the bars. In China, you're considered an adult at the age of sixteen. We all know that the teen years can be the worst; you're not a child anymore, but you're not quite an adult yet, either. I think it's even harder on her, because she's Chinese. She's treated like an adult in China, but in America, she's a child.

XXII: Into the Future

We were back from China and back into our daily routines when I received another letter from her school saying that she was behind in her schoolwork again. She'd turned in only one unit since returning from China.

I was very surprised; I'd thought Yvonne had come back from China in a better frame of mind. She'd cleaned up her room and was pretty much staying home most of the time.

Cleaning up her room had truly been a big deal. Her room had been in terrible condition. I was always finding dirty dishes, and I had no idea how she knew which clothes were clean and which were dirty. Her clothes were everywhere, from the bathroom to the closet. But now she'd done a complete 180, cleaning everything from top to bottom without my saying a word. I was shocked. I'd been forever telling her to clean up her room, and she'd barely touch it. Now it was spotless, and I hadn't asked her to do anything.

I never know what she's thinking. Instead of being glad she'd cleaned her room, I was concerned that something might be wrong with her.

Since coming back from China, I've been wondering what she does in that room. She can have it completely clean, and then I'll see it later the same day, and it's completely trashed. It might stay that way for a week, or two—who knows. Then she'll clean everything up and keep it that way for a week or so. Then she'll trash it again. She just confuses me.

When I sat her down to ask why she was behind on her schoolwork again, she insisted she wasn't behind. This was on a Friday. Monday morning, I took her to school and went inside with her to talk to her teacher. Her teacher said Yvonne had turned in four units the week before and that she was actually ahead for the month. She told me Yvonne had been behind when the notice was mailed, but she had caught up now. This made me very happy. The last thing I needed was her falling behind in her schoolwork again or getting into any trouble.

I'm never sure what's going on with my daughter. Sometimes she does everything perfectly, and other times she seems to just throw her hands up and not care. It's the same with her attitude. She can be so sweet and understanding about some things, but then a few minutes later, she's just full of bad attitude. When she starts with her bad attitude, most of the time she's funny to me.

One day I realized that she's been involved in entertainment for so long that it seems completely normal to her. She's such a professional, and it just comes naturally—she doesn't see herself as anything special. But I see her as something special, and her family knows how special she is, and we've tried to do a good job of nurturing her talent.

I asked her once if she gets nervous when she sees so many girls showing up for an audition. "Mom, if it's meant to happen, I'll get the part," she said. "If not, oh well; there will be another audition."

She told me she wasn't going to rely on a career in entertainment; she's going to college. She also said she wasn't going to quit acting until she feels like she's had enough. I think she has a really good attitude about it and seems to have a good grip on what's going on around her.

Yvonne kept mentioning to me that she couldn't see things far away, but I thought she was just looking for a new fashion statement. She can be like that. She'd been taking the lenses out of my sunglasses, even my prescription glasses, and wearing them that way since she was ten years old. Later, she'd even buy expensive glasses, take the lenses out, and wear them. Then I noticed her squinting her eyes trying to read a street sign in the car one day. I took her to have her eyes examined and found out she needed glasses. Most people would be upset to find out they have to wear glasses, but she was so happy. I was happy too. Now she finally had a reason to wear them.

At the beginning of February 2010, she got her certificate of completion in driver's education. She'd been working on this for over a month. She was very happy, but I was very upset; I kept this to myself, though. To me it was just one step closer to her becoming an adult. Once she had her own license and her own car, she'd be gone all the time. Plus, there were all the dangers that go along with driving, not to mention the expenses. It's hard to let your kid grow up.

When Valentine's Day came around that year, she brought me some flowers, a big heart balloon, and some chocolate. I was so surprised; it was the first gift she'd gotten for me in a long time. When she was little, she'd always given me handmade Valentine's and Christmas cards. But she hadn't done anything like that in a while.

February 25, 2010, was a big day for us: we were informed that I'd been invited to an awards ceremony for the movie *Still the Drums*. Yvonne wasn't invited to the ceremony because of her age. I mentioned before that this was a film in which we played mother and daughter in the summer of 2007.

"Are you kidding me? I'm in the movie," she said in a tone that let me know right away that she was upset.

"They're going to be serving alcohol there, baobao," I told her.

"I don't want any alcohol!" she said. "What does that have to do with me?"

"They don't want you drinking alcohol."

"But I don't want any alcohol," she screamed.

I finally explained it to her, and when she understood, she thought it was stupid. "I don't want to go anyway," she said.

Three years later, I'd forgotten we'd even played those roles. I guess that's show business. It turns out the movie is complete and winning some outstanding awards. Talbot Perry Simons has won six awards for this movie. It's his first film. The awards have included best film, best actor, best song, best feature film directorial debut, and best screenplay. This ceremony was for New York's International Independent Film and Video Festival.

When I attended the awards ceremony, Talbot, the director, who also wrote the screenplay, said to me, "I'm so happy to have you and your daughter in my movie. You're both up-and-coming stars."

Through this movie, Yvonne and I have gotten quite a bit of extra promotion online and in the real world. After I attended the awards ceremony, several pictures showed up on different websites of me standing beside the banner for the movie. That was a big surprise. I was also in several entertainment articles.

When Yvonne and I were in China, I had all kinds of phone problems. Before we left the States, I went to a T-Mobile location and told them exactly what I'd be doing. They told me there would not be a problem. They said all I had to do was go to a ChinaMobil location with my phone when I got to China. They'd put a new SIM card in my phone, and it would work. That way, I wouldn't have to sign a new contract in China. Oh, if it had only been that easy. It didn't work that way at all.

When we arrived in China, before I ever got the chance to go to a ChinaMobil location, my phone would not work. When I got to a ChinaMobil location, they couldn't get it to work, either. When I spoke to T-Mobile in the United States, they told me there was nothing they could do until I got back to the States.

Needless to say, I had a very difficult time staying in touch with Yvonne's management, my agent, my husband, and my company. All my business and personal affairs were in shambles by the time we got home. I did manage to talk to my husband and Yvonne's manager while we were there, but this cost me a lot of money, since I had to use a public phone. I couldn't even check my messages until I got back to Burbank.

The first thing I did when we walked in the door was check messages. I had a lot of them. There was one from a theater in Chinatown. They wanted Yvonne and me to play mother and daughter in a production they were working on. We'd worked with them the year before. They liked us so much that they were inviting us back again.

I was excited; it was another chance to do a role on the same stage as Yvonne. The year before, I'd been in a completely different scene. This time, we were going to be doing a scene where a single mother was arguing with her troubled teen daughter about her bad attitude. "You two should have no problems with this at all," my friend said. "It's like a scene out of your daily lives."

We all laughed; that was pretty funny. And we did the scene perfectly.

Both of us were very busy at the time. It's all volunteer work at that theater, and they had a lot of rehearsals. We went to the first two, but we didn't make the next two. I wanted to make more of the rehearsals, since it was a chance for Yvonne to get better at speaking Chinese. Everyone there speaks nothing but Chinese to one another all day. They kept calling, wanting to know if we were going to make the next one.

"Do you have your part together?" I asked her. "They want to know if we're going to make any of the other rehearsals before the show."

"I've got my part together, Mom," she said, "as long as you've got yours."

"Are you sure?" I asked. "You don't need me to go over any of your lines with you?" That's the way I am. I'm always checking and double checking her. But that's a mother's job, right?

"Mom, I've already told you five times," she said, in that agitated voice that makes me laugh. Because that's the way she is when she thinks I'm pushing too much or just aggravating her.

My best friend told me I do it because I like her expression when she gets angry. It could be true; I do think she's cute when she's angry.

I called the theater back and told them we were very busy but would be there opening day for the final rehearsal. I asked them if this was going to be a problem, and it wasn't. I have to say, it was so easy working with the people at the Chinese theater. I'd be glad to work with them in the future. Both times we've been there, it was a wonderful experience and a fantastic show.

With the new hair extensions I'd gotten in China, I landed a part in a John Mayer video. I don't really know if it was because of my hair or not, but I liked my new look. It was my first music video. I was a bridesmaid in a wedding, for the song "Half of My Heart." It was really different from anything I'd done in the past. The production, the pace of the shooting, everything was different. I loved it, and right after that, I got a part in another music video. This one was for a Spanish artist. I had to stand there, acting like I was singing the song into my cell phone in Spanish. I don't even speak English that well; I have a heavy accent. It was pretty difficult and took more than one take, believe me, but I managed to do it.

Every time I run into a challenge like that, it makes me appreciate Yvonne more. Have you ever watched somebody doing something really difficult, and they just make it look easy? That's what it's like watching Yvonne work. She's like somebody who shoots basketball really well, with that smooth, fluid motion, like everything is going to fall right into place. I really enjoy watching her work.

A lot happened for us really fast. We were both working again, even though Hollywood was still very slow. Yvonne had become SAG eligible, which means she could get into the actors' union. My friend and I started talking about her having an entertainment attorney, someone who knows about all these things. I don't know what the right time is for her to join the union. I'm SAG eligible, but I haven't joined yet. I'm not trying to have a career in acting, though. These are important decisions that could affect her career.

Weeks had passed since we'd been in China, and I hadn't spoken to a lot of people I'd normally speak to regularly. One of them is Yvonne's old guitar teacher. He lives in Texas now, but he lived in Hollywood for many years. He's a performing musician. He called on the same evening that we'd been talking about Yvonne's career. Since I knew he was a professional musician, has always been interested in Yvonne's activities, and really believes in her, I asked him what he thought about the idea of her joining the union or getting an attorney.

He told me he had a friend who works for a law firm in Beverly Hills. He said his friend was an attorney, but not in the field of entertainment. He said his friend might have a referral for me, though.

The next day, his attorney friend contacted me and asked if Yvonne had a demo reel. He said he had an associate who works for one of the largest talent agencies in Hollywood. I didn't even know what a demo reel was. I just told him I'd talk with her management and get back to him. I hadn't expected everything to happen that fast.

I immediately contacted her management and asked what a demo reel was and how hard it would be to get one for Yvonne. They gave me the names of four different demo reel companies in the Los Angeles area. Yvonne and I looked at each of their websites and made a choice. I had no idea it was going to cost so much. None of them were cheap.

Let me tell you what a demo reel is. It's basically two or three scenes on DVD that show your acting abilities. It shouldn't be commercial material; it should be scenes from a feature film. We didn't have any of the footage from any of the films Yvonne had been in, so we had to come up with scenes from scratch. The producer at the demo reel company will write scenes for you and shoot the scenes. They can even provide a makeup artist and actors to act with you in your scenes. But all of this costs extra.

When you're famous or just a working entertainer and things are written about you or you do a part in a film, it's up to you and your team to track that stuff down. They never send you a copy of the movie or the article.

We chose to do two scenes from scratch, plus still shots, and include footage from the documentary she did that airs in China. Instead of the producer writing the scenes, though, Yvonne said she could write them. She said that way it would cost less. I wasn't sure if she'd be able to do it, but I told her to give it a shot.

We did end up paying for a makeup artist and two actors to act with her in the scenes. The demo reel turned out great in the end. The first scene she wrote was a murder scene. She was the murderer, of course. The second scene was a comedy like Disney or Nickelodeon, also written by my brilliant young one.

Once we had her demo reel in hand, we hand-delivered a copy to the talent agency. The very next morning, I got an e-mail from them saying they wanted to meet with Yvonne right away. I was thrilled; you never hear back from these people that fast. We hadn't even gotten the demo reel to them until the evening of the day before. I thought for sure this was the moment that would change everything for her.

I think even she got excited about this one. Signing with an agency like that could mean the end of going to dead-end, nowhere auditions, which would save me a lot of money and a lot of time. Also, she'd have a large, reputable company representing her. When she went for an audition, they'd be speaking for her before she ever arrived. That can make all the difference in the world.

We set up the meeting, but we were so disappointed to find out that although they were very interested in Yvonne, they were going through personnel and structural changes within their company. They told her they'd contact her in the future. This is how it is in entertainment. The highs and lows are incredible.

Hollywood has been so screwed up since the economy went south. A lot of people have lost their jobs, and studios and production houses have closed. A lot of the talent agencies have downsized. It's not just Hollywood; the business at my convenient store in Texas has slowed way down. The talent agencies are always changing personnel. Sometimes as soon as you make contact with someone, they stop working there or move to a new department. It's a lot to keep up with.

Even though it's been slow, Yvonne and I both still like to work. We'll take parts that don't pay, but it has to be a part we're really interested in. For instance, I recently played a role in a film called *Mahjong*. *Mahjong* is a traditional Chinese game, kind of like dominos. I played a mother who was addicted to playing *mahjong* online. I had a lot of fun playing this part. I also ran into a friend there, Jessica, who I'd worked with in the past. She'd played my mother in a commercial for California Telephone Access. It was good to see her again. Since then, we've become really good friends.

On Mother's Day, there was a screening for *Mahjong*. Yvonne went with me, and we had a lot of fun. I had a great time showing off my adorable daughter. Everyone wanted to talk to her about her experiences in China. The crowd was mostly Chinese, so they knew all about *Journey to the West*. Like I said before, the director is very famous in China. It was a really big deal to all of them that she'd been in two episodes of *Journey to the West*. After the screening, Yvonne took me out to dinner for Mother's

Day, and she had a special gift for me. I love her so much. She always has a way of surprising me. That was a great Mother's Day.

My friend Jessica is not only an actress; she also writes and directs. When she met Yvonne, she said she had a part for her in a feature film she was working on. Yvonne did the part, and once again we kind of forgot about it and moved on.

A few months passed, and Jessica called saying she'd finished the film, called *I Love You Daddy*. She said her only problem was that she had no location yet for the screening. I wasn't sure what she was looking for, but I told her my housing complex had a clubhouse. All I had to do was reserve it ahead of time. I told her it had a wide-screen TV, a full kitchen, and plenty of seating, even a pool table. She came by to look it over, and we agreed on a date.

The only problem was that the day she wanted to do it was the day after I'd scheduled a photo shoot for Yvonne and me so we could get some new headshots. I had a makeup artist coming and everything. I'd planned wardrobe changes, location changes, the whole nine yards. I knew it was going to be a long day. On top of that, my birthday was the day after the date she'd chosen. Tony was coming to town the morning of the screening. I thought, *How am I going to pull all this off?*

The day of the photo shoot, I had so many things to deal with. I knew that the photographer and the makeup artist would be there all day. I had to figure out what we were going to eat for lunch and dinner. I decided I'd set everything up in the clubhouse, since we were using it the next day for the movie screening. I had to take everything from upstairs in my house to the clubhouse, including food, dishes, clothing, and so on.

I got a friend to help me. We'd recently started a new business together, buying and selling classic and antique cars. We'd purchased a 1940 Packard—it needed to be restored, but it was running. What a beautiful car! We'd found it in a barn in Santa Barbara. Part of the plan was to drive the car somewhere and take some pictures of Yvonne and me dressed as flapper girls from the 1920s.

We pulled that off, and the pictures turned out great. We went to a local park and took a lot of shots there. We got a lot of good pictures that day. It was a long day, though. By the time the photographer and makeup artist left, it was around 8:00 p.m.

Then Jessica showed up to talk over things for the movie screening the next afternoon. We talked and laughed for a while, catching up. I don't see her that often; we're both very busy. She left around 11:30 p.m. I was exhausted and knew that Tony was flying in the next morning around 8:00 a.m.

I went upstairs, and talked to Yvonne for a few minutes. Then I told her, "Good-night, baobao. Mama's tired."

It was another thirty minutes or so before I finally went to bed, so it was probably 12:30 or 1:00 a.m. I fell asleep as soon as my head hit the pillow and didn't wake up until I heard the alarm the next morning. It sounded like it was a million miles away. When I finally woke up, I had the biggest hangover. I hardly drink, but I'd had two beers while talking with Jessica.

I stumbled around my room, trying to remember why I'd set the alarm. All at once it dawned on me, and I thought, *He's coming. Tony's flying in this morning. I've got to pick him up at the airport.* At this point, I'd already been up for ten or fifteen minutes, so I had to get a move on.

"Yvonne, get up—we've got to pick your dad up at the airport," I yelled down the hall. I heard nothing. I waited. "Yvonne, Yvonne!" I yelled louder.

"What do you want, Mom?" I finally heard her say.

"We've got to pick Tony up at the airport," I told her. "And you need to get your things together for school. We'll have to take you straight there after picking him up."

I heard her moaning and mumbling as she rolled out of bed. "Are you sure that's today, Mom?" she asked.

Needless to say, we were late again.

Once I picked Tony up from the airport, I didn't lie down again until everyone left after the screening. The guests were supposed to start arriving around 4:00 p.m. Saturday night. On Sunday, we'd have to clean up the clubhouse. I was already tired, and I'd just gotten out of bed.

Tony was flying in just for my birthday. I knew the last thing he'd want to do was help me set up all this stuff and deal with all the people who were coming. I had no choice, though. Everything was already set. Besides, I'd warned him before he booked his flight that Yvonne and I were very busy.

After we picked him up at the airport, we drove straight to Yvonne's school to drop her off; she was already late. Then Tony and I ate breakfast, and he jumped right into the frenzy with my friend. I have to say, they really made everything a breeze. I was so worried about getting it all set up in time.

I was overwhelmed by the number of people who showed up that day. Everyone loved the movie, a horror film. Yvonne was at her father's and had said she wasn't going to be there, but she showed up just before they started the movie. She'd gotten her father to drive her all the way back home, which is over an hour's drive. These days, she sees her father regularly; she doesn't see it as a punishment anymore. I hardly even talk to him. She calls and sets up a time for him to pick her up. I used to be the one trying to get the two of them together; now I don't have anything to do with it at all.

"I thought you weren't coming," I said.

"I realized," she told me, "that this might be the last time I see some of these people."

I thought it was a good thing she was there. I was really impressed with the way she handled herself that night. She'd even invited a couple of her friends. After the screening, they hung out and played pool.

Tony fell asleep on the couch during the movie. In fact, he slept right there for most of the evening. He'd been up since 4:00 a.m. Houston time. He was so comfortable, and I was so tired. Every time I looked at him, I envied him. I still have a really good relationship with Tony, even though we don't see each other that often now that Yvonne and I have moved to California. He's such a good man, though, and has always been so supportive.

People from the movie were there, and after the screening, everyone hung around, talking, shooting pool, and eating. I'd made traditional Chinese tea eggs and dumplings. Other people had brought food, beer, and wine. It was a great time. I didn't go to sleep until 5:00 or 6:00 the next morning. People were still hanging around at 4:30 a.m. I'd call that a successful screening. Everybody had a great time. Jessica was really pleased with the outcome.

Recently, I'd made arrangements for Yvonne and me to make another trip to China. The producer who got her the part in *Journey to the West* said that there were more opportunities for her in China, and he'd like to help make them happen.

First, though, he said she needed to improve her Chinese. I told him this was something she'd been working on. He said there was an acting school in Beijing, and that if I took her there, it would help her with her acting and her Chinese. I signed both of us up. I thought it would be great for us to take the class together, and it would be a good way for her to learn to speak proper Chinese. Plus, it was another opportunity for her to see China.

Right after I signed us up for the classes, she auditioned for a Verizon commercial. There were so many beautiful young teenage girls there. I didn't think Yvonne had a chance, how were they going to notice her out of all of those girls. But she got a callback. Then they called the next day, saying she was on hold with another girl. She also was called for a new TV show being done by Nickelodeon. I could see another dilemma coming.

The next day, my friend asked me if I had my life to live all over again, would I make the same choices, or was there anything I would change. "My husband just asked me the same question last week," I told her. "Moving to California with Yvonne and leaving him in Texas has put a lot of strain on my marriage, and Yvonne has been influenced in a lot of ways that she wouldn't have been in Texas. Some good, some bad."

"So what's your answer?" my friend asked.

"I've lost a lot of money since moving to Hollywood, and it hasn't been easy raising Yvonne as basically a single mother through her teenage years," I told her. "You know, Yvonne is not a normal kid. But even with all the hassles, all the expenses, and all the stress, the answer is no, I wouldn't change a thing."

"That's what I thought your answer would be," my friend said.

My daughter will be turning sixteen years old soon. She's been so many places and has experienced so many things, more than a lot of people do in their whole lifetimes. I think she's been very blessed, and I've been blessed to have her in my life.

I never intended to be an actress or even do any print work or have anything to do with entertainment. When I was younger, living in China, I'd considered the idea, and was once even approached by a modeling agency. But in China at that time, my parents just didn't take this idea seriously. Well, you know my story now. It just wasn't like that in China back then.

I thought it was kind of funny when I was first asked to read for a commercial and then got accepted for the part. I'd thought that my time was over. I was concentrating on youthful Yvonne. I would never have been part of any of this if it wasn't for her. I've had so much fun with the work I've done, and it's been a joy watching her work.

The first commercial I got was for OfficeMax. When I went for the first audition, a couple of hundred people were there. It was right before Christmas in 2006. I'll never forget this. We'd been living in California for only a couple of months. I was told it was for a Christmas promotion. After the audition, I was told, "Thank you. You can go." Then I got called back for a second audition. This time, about fifty people were there. Once again, I was told, "Thank you. You can go." No, wait a minute—I think the second time they said, "Thank you for coming. You can go."

A few days went by, and they called again. I almost didn't go; I was getting annoyed. This time, it was down to about twenty people. "This is the final audition," they told us. "Each of you will walk into the next room one at a time, where you'll find a large gift box. You are to lift the lid, reach in, and get yourself a free gift from OfficeMax, and then proceed through the door on the other side of the room."

When I walked into the room, no one was in there but me. That made me nervous. Then they shut the door behind me. When I heard the door close, I got scared. I thought, *Oh, my God, what's going to happen?* I saw the gift box sitting on the floor in the middle of the room. I walked up to the box. When I lifted the lid to get my free gift, a midget jumped out yelling, "Merry Christmas!" There were no gifts. They were filming the whole time to see different people's reactions. I guess they liked my reaction, because I got the job.

When I walked through the other door, ten or fifteen people were standing there, including all of the crew, the director, and the producer. They were all laughing hysterically at me. Later, when I watched the footage, I laughed too. There wasn't a sound coming out of my mouth, and they were obviously laughing at the expression on my face. But when I looked in that box, I have to tell you, I was terrified. I thought I was going to have a heart attack.

I was so happy about getting the job. It was the easiest job I've ever done in my life. That was the job. They told me they'd be sending me a check in the mail.

On my way home, I started thinking about my daughter and all the auditions she'd been through. It hasn't been easy for her at all. There have been plenty of times when she was on hold for a job but didn't get it, and even more times when she didn't get called back at all. I regretted telling her about all the holds. I could have just waited until she got the job. But when we went to some of these auditions, so many girls were there. I wanted her to know she was one of the final choices.

It was hard to watch her deal with so much rejection at such a young age. She'd always say something like, "They were looking for a certain type of girl, and I just didn't fit." But sometimes I could see her disappointment.

She's changed a lot since she's gotten older, and she seems to handle it all very well. She's always handled it well. When I started going to auditions, I had a whole new appreciation for what my little girl had been going through. Now I really saw that she was a natural. She never showed fear, nervousness, or disappointment. She had the attitude of a professional actress.

Many times, when I think I did well and then don't get called back, I feel very disappointed. It's even worse when I get called back or put on hold, only to not get the job in the end. All that excitement just falls out from under you. It's hard to not be excited about the idea of having some of these parts. This happens all the time. These days, Yvonne never even seems that excited when she does get the part. I'm glad I've been through the audition process many times now. I've been on the sets and worked in entertainment in several different ways. It has helped me understand exactly what Yvonne has been up against.

She takes each audition very seriously and always memorizes her lines very quickly. Many times, her management has suggested that she go to an acting coach before going for an audition. Yvonne is so confident in herself that she's used a coach only two or three times, and only after I pushed her into it. Sometimes I wonder if she's just trying to save me money; she knows coaches are expensive. The times she has used a coach, however, she didn't even get the job.

By the way, she did get the nationwide Verizon commercial. The shoot was held in beautiful Malibu, California, right by the Pacific Ocean.

When I started writing this book, I thought I'd tell my life story: loves lost, dreams never obtained. When I look it over, however, I see that it's mostly about Yvonne. Since the day she was born, she's been my life story. I also realize that I've cried a lot of tears in my lifetime. Just think, though: if I hadn't brought Chang Lu to America, the world would have been robbed of Yvonne.

I can't wait to see what she does next.

Two Chinese flapper girls

Epilogue: Poems Written by My Father

Say good-bye

Three bicycles leave Kaifeng at dawn

Only two will return

Cold wind blows as they pass the third ancient wall

Even though they have traveled so far

They must still say good-bye

Outside of the city they can go no further

The wife and the child must return home

Remaining in the east while he travels west

They wave good-bye

As they watch his back ride away smaller and smaller

送别：

晓行离汴京、爱妻送归程、

清晨凉风爽，驱车到城堤、

千里终有别、劳燕复西东、

举手长劳劳、依稀看背影。

举头新月白，往事忆朦胧。

Halfway

Coming into the small village of Xinhua

The early sun has rose

Daylight now and the roosters crow

When my bike crosses the next bridge

Pass the river to the town of Zhongmu

I will know I'm halfway

I see the sun rise

And all the peach blossoms in bloom

All of the birds sing

As the farmers start their day

途中:

鸡鸣杏花月、车迹板桥村,

驱车近中牟 晓阳冉冉昇、

桃花红似火、百鸟竞争鸣、

斜径通幽处、林深有村民。

Arriving in Zhengzhou

Past ancient Guandu villages

Almost there

I hear the leaves of the poplar trees

Rustling in the wind

Telling me welcome back to Zhengzhou

The leaves are clapping

The magpies are singing

Welcome welcome

Once again 140 miles

Three hours later

How do you do this every weekend

I am one with my bike and we are as light as a feather

抵郑：

朝辞古汴京、驱车过官渡、

杨树拍手笑、喜鹊跳相迎、

行程一百四、用时3点钟、

问君何能尔　体健车自轻。

About the Authors

Grace and Sames are both entertainers who reside in the Burbank area of California.

Grace has been on television shows including *1000 Ways to Die* and the hit series *24*, as well as in music videos for artists John Mayer and Bunbury. She has performed in theaters and on radio and has done print work and voiceover work. She also appears in the movie *Still the Drums* along with her daughter, Yvonne Lu, playing mother and daughter. This film has won many awards.

Sames is a songwriter and vocalist who has been performing on stages from the East Coast to the West Coast of the United States since he was seventeen years old. He has had several songs published. He has also appeared in two independent films, as well as on radio and television. He has performed at all of the top clubs on the Sunset Strip. He has won awards through the media in Hollywood.

Words of Praise

It's been a real pleasure working with Grace and Yvonne and an honor to be asked to comment on this book. I found both Grace and Yvonne to be consummate performers who are very dedicated to their craft. I look forward to working with them in the future. Their lives have been full of adventure, giving them a lot to share. Grace's book has an interesting perspective and was a very enjoyable read. I highly recommend it to everyone.

—Talbot Perry Simons, producer, writer, director, actor

Immigration has become a phenomenal part of our civilization, part of our culture, fusing mankind, merging humanity through many generations. Bringing us talents that the world would have never known otherwise. The main character in this literary work is a hero to her family and her country. Traveling from East to West, from a little girl of Chinese descent to a young Hollywood star. Through the course of her life, it has not only been her hard work and struggles, but also her family, who have made many sacrifices in order to bring her this far. The spirit and ambition of several generations have been handed down, making the family and even the Chinese nation stronger.

The main theme of the twenty-first century has been Eastern and Western cultures merging, making our planet smaller than ever before. Yvonne has managed to have an influence in both China and America.

—Linda Chen, Chinese American author

It is nice to see a mother put in so much effort to help her daughter with her career. I've always enjoyed the colorful fonts that Grace chooses to use in her e-mails to me. I think this book is a wonderful idea, and a great way for Yvonne and her mother to introduce themselves to the world and for Yvonne to learn about her heritage.

—Betty McCormick, talent manager, Midwest Talent

Hollywood has always been the world's center for film making. It is my hope that more young Chinese will find their way to Hollywood, and let their talents shine.

—Wen Jiang, actor, director, writer

I feel like this book could be a road map for other parents with children who strive for a life in the world of entertainment.
—Qing Yan, chairman/CEO, International American Media Group